MAKE THAT GRADE ORGANISATIONAL BEHAVIOUR

SECOND EDITION

Michèle Kehoe

GILL & MACMILLAN

Gill & Macmillan
Hume Avenue
Park West
Dublin 12
with associated companies throughout the world
www.gillmacmillan.ie

978 07171 5633 7

Print origination in Ireland by O'K Graphic Design, Dublin

The paper used in this book is made from the wood pulp of managed forests. For every tree felled, at least one tree is planted, thereby renewing natural resources.

A CIP catalogue record for this book is available from the British Library.

To Sophie, Michael and Julian
Every day is a learning day

CONTENTS

Contents

1
INTRODUCTION TO ORGANISATIONAL BEHAVIOUR

Objectives

This chapter will help you to:

- Describe the nature of organisational behaviour.
- Understand the goals of organisational behaviour.
- Appreciate the benefits of understanding the behaviour of people in the workplace.

1.1 Organisational behaviour defined

Organisational behaviour is the study of organisations and the people who work in them.

People tend to take the influence that organisations have on their lives for granted, even though they affect everything that people do. Organisations have a very significant and powerful effect on individuals. People are educated by organisations, buy food and clothing and many other goods and services from organisations, work in organisations and are regulated by government organisations. Therefore, the relationships that people have with organisations include being an employee, a customer, a competitor, a supplier, an owner and/or an investor. How many organisations have had an effect on you today?

Moorhead and Griffin (2012) have defined organisational behaviour as:

> **the study of human behaviour in organisational settings, the interface between human behaviour and the organisation, and the organisation itself.**

According to Buchanan and Huczynski (2010), organisational behaviour is **'the study of the structure, functioning and performance of organizations and the behaviour of groups and individuals within them'.** The aim of organisational behaviour is to achieve a better understanding of human behaviour in organisations, thereby enhancing the effectiveness of organisations. An understanding of organisational behaviour is both critical and central to the task of management.

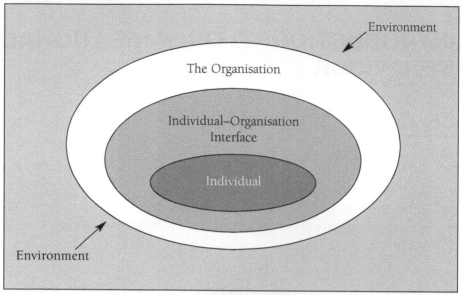

Figure 1.1 The areas of study in organisational behaviour

The study of **organisational behaviour (OB)** can be divided into three parts:

1. **Individual processes in organisations** – The focus of this aspect of OB is on the individual employee and their personal characteristics, experiences and background. Areas under investigation include perception, attitudes, learning, personality, motivation and stress. An insight into these individual processes provides an understanding of the reasons why people behave the way they do in the workplace. The importance of understanding why people behave the way they do is fundamental to the study of OB. As stated by Buchanan and Huczynski (2010), 'organizations do not "behave". Only people can be said to behave.'

2. **Interpersonal processes in organisations** – This area of OB examines the impact that the individual has on the organisation and that the organisation has on the individual. At this level, the focus of the study of organisational behaviour is on the dynamics of interaction between managers and co-workers and on formal policies and procedures. Aspects of study include group dynamics and teamwork, leadership, conflict and communication.

3. **Organisational processes** – Organisations exist before and after individuals join and leave them and groups are formed and disband. At this level of analysis, the structure and functioning of the organisation is

examined. Areas for consideration include organisational design, organisational change and development and organisational culture.

The study of the behaviour of organisations and the people within them is very interesting, complex and dynamic. It is important that the environment or context in which the organisation exists is considered at all times. The environment will present opportunities and threats. Organisations are influenced by social, cultural, physical, political and economic environments. In order to be effective, an organisation must have an insight into the current and future environment in which it operates.

1.2 Goals of organisational behaviour

The goals of organisational behaviour are:

*   To *explain* the factors that influence the behaviour of people in the workplace.
*   To *make predictions* about the consequences of particular types of behaviour.
*   To *control* the behaviour of employees to improve organisational effectiveness.

Buchanan and Huczynski (2010) have defined **organisations** *as social arrangements for achieving controlled performance in undertaking collective goals.* An organisation is a group of people who are arranged and managed to achieve collective goals. Organisations are made up of people: some workplaces consist of a few employees, others many. Employees communicate with one another to undertake their tasks. They work together to achieve the shared objectives and collective goals of the organisation. In the workplace employees cannot do what they want to, when and how they want to do it; they must follow the rules and regulations. Their performances are therefore controlled. Employees are informed about what time to start and end work, the required uniform, the nature of the task to be undertaken and their roles and responsibilities. Controlled performance leads to the effective and efficient functioning of the organisation.

The concept of control is central to the success of an organisation. It is also the factor that distinguishes an organisation from other social groups. Control involves:

*   Setting performance standards, such as attendance rates, the quality and quantity of production, customer service levels.

- Measuring actual performance by monitoring the behaviour of employees.
- Comparing standard performance with actual performance.
- Taking corrective action, if necessary, such as providing additional staff training and development programmes, revising pay rates, redesigning jobs, implementing new policies and procedures.

1.3 Study of organisational behaviour

The study of organisational behaviour emerged as a result of a combination of a number of disciplines within the social sciences, including:

- **Psychology** – The focus of psychology is on understanding the behaviour of individuals in a variety of environments. Research in this area has made a significant contribution to our understanding of areas such as learning, personality and stress.
- **Sociology** – This involves the study of society and human social interaction and has provided an insight into patterns of social relationships, social action and culture.
- **Political science** – Through the study of the political arena, an understanding of power and organisational politics is gained.
- **Management** – The aim of management is to make the most efficient use of human and material resources. Research in this area has led to an understanding of the different approaches to management that have been adopted and the value and contributions that these approaches have made to modern organisations.

The study of organisational behaviour is rich and dynamic. The areas under investigation are like a tapestry. Each part is woven into the next and plays a role in providing an understanding of the performance of an organisation at a particular time. Organisations are made up of parts which interconnect. Each person has an effect on and is affected by each other person. The formation of groups influences the nature of interaction and the experience of working in a particular organisation. Organisational factors such as change and culture have a strong overriding influence on the individuals and the groups that make up the workforce. Finally, it is very important to consider the impact of the external operating environment on the organisation.

To fully understand the behaviour of people at work, the whole picture needs to be seen and appreciated: the factors relating to the individual; the individual as part of a group; the group as part of a wider organisation and the organisation as part of the environment. Therefore, the study of organisational behaviour is complex, but very exciting.

Over the years, research into organisational behaviour has focused on many questions, but due to the diversity of people, the range of their experiences and the fact that no two workplaces are exactly the same, few definitive answers to these questions have been arrived at. The questions asked include:

- What causes employees to behave the way they do?
- What motivates employees?
- Why do some people perform better than others?
- How does stress affect people in the workplace?
- Can conflict benefit an organisation?
- What is the most effective style of leadership?

1.4 Conclusion

The continuing challenge of organisational behaviour is to understand people and to meet the wide range of human needs in the workplace. The increasing complexity of the global environment presents an ongoing need to enhance our understanding of the interactions between people and the implications for the functioning of the organisation. Other challenges and opportunities for managers today to use OB concepts are examined by Robbins *et al.* (2010); these include managing workforce diversity, improving quality and productivity, stimulating innovation and change, helping employees balance work–life conflicts and improving ethical behaviour.

The fact that there is *no one best way* to understand and describe social interaction may be a cause of frustration for some, but for others it opens up endless possibilities for further research. The study of organisational behaviour asks many questions and presents few definitive answers, but importantly provides alternative ways of thinking about issues that arise in organisations. As you study the areas of organisational behaviour, you will gradually gain an insight into the many factors that cause people to behave the way they do. Upon completion of this course in organisational behaviour your learning will continue and become consolidated in real-life experience. Enjoy the journey of learning presented by the organisational world around you and remember that every day is a learning day.

Summary

- Definition of organisational behaviour (OB).
- Goals of OB.
- Emergence of the study of OB.
- Importance of understanding OB.

Theory to real life

1. What organisations affect you on a daily basis? How do these organisations influence the way you think, feel and behave?
2. How do organisations influence employees?
3. How do employees influence organisations?
4. In what way is the behaviour of employees controlled by organisations?
5. Why is controlled performance important in organisations?

Exercises

1. After each class write down three things that you learned during the lecture or tutorial.
2. **Before vs. After:**
   - As you commence your studies in OB, take note of the knowledge, skills and abilities or *tools* that managers require to effectively manage the behaviour of employees.
   - Then, when you have completed the course, think about all the knowledge, skills and abilities or *tools* that you can now bring to the workplace to assist you in being an effective co-worker, employee, manager and/or leader.
   - You knew a lot about OB from your life experiences, but during the OB course you learned about many different theories, their application in the workplace and the different styles and approaches that can be used to effectively manage people in organisations.

Essay questions

1. Describe the nature of organisational behaviour.
2. Examine the benefits of the study of organisational behaviour.

Short questions

1. Organisational behaviour examines the reasons people _____ the way they do in the workplace.
2. According to Buchanan and Huczynski (2010), organisations are social arrangements for the controlled performance of collective goals. Which of these elements is a unique feature of organisations?
3. Identify three factors influencing individual behaviour in organisations.
4. What are the three goals of organisational behaviour?
5. The study of organisational behaviour can be divided into the following three parts:
   a. _____ process
   b. _____ process
   c. _____ process

2
PERCEPTION

Objectives

This chapter will help you to:

- Describe the nature of perception and sensation.
- Understand the process of perception.
- Explain errors in person perception.
- Identify the general sources of errors and remedies in social perception.
- Provide examples of how behaviour is affected by perceptions.

2.1 Perception defined

The way people perceive their environment influences their behaviour in the workplace. It directly affects how people interact with and react to their environment. **Perception** is an active, dynamic, cognitive process that helps individuals to make sense of the information that they receive from the world around them. Perception is an individual, subjective process and is influenced by factors such as attitudes, values, expectations and motives. It is therefore impossible to avoid bias. Each person's perception of reality shapes the way they think, feel and behave. We perceive the world around us in different ways.

The subjective nature of the perceptual process was commented on with great insight by the philosopher and psychologist William James (1842–1910) when he stated that:

> part of what we perceive comes through our senses from the object before us, another part...always comes out of our own mind. (James, 1890)

Perception can be defined as:

> **The psychological processes through which people receive, organise and interpret information from the environment** (Atkinson et al., 1993).

> **A complex process by which people select, organise and interpret sensory stimulation into a meaningful picture of the world** (Markin, 1974).

The process of *sensation* is fundamental to perception. Sensation is the immediate and direct response of the sensory organs to simple stimuli (MacDonagh *et al.*, 2002). Sensation involves the relatively unprocessed result of stimulation of sensory receptors in the eyes, ears, nose, tongue and skin. A sensory experience is finite and creates an immediate response to stimuli. In contrast, perception involves constant interpretation of sensory information and related responses. Without the ability to organise and interpret sensations, the world would appear to be a meaningless jumble of colours, shapes and sounds. Without any perceptual ability, an individual would not be able to recognise faces or understand language.

In theory, the processes of sensation and perception are very distinct, yet complementary. In practice, the processes of sensation and perception are virtually impossible to separate as they are part of one continuous process.

2.2 Process of perception

It is impossible to process all the information that is available to the senses. To prevent total bombardment of the senses, individuals constantly and actively select significant stimuli (such as people, objects and events) and filter out information that is not relevant. This is called **selective attention**. The process of perceptual selectivity results in behaviour that is not in accordance with reality but with how the world is perceived.

A boundary point has been identified between the sensory information that we can and cannot detect. The point between sensing and not sensing information is called the **perceptual threshold**. Once this point or threshold has been crossed we can, for example, hear, see and taste stimuli and therefore have a sensory experience. This threshold level varies among individuals and is affected by factors such as their physical condition, motivational state, training and experience.

As we are all bombarded by information from the world around us on a daily basis, it is important to remember that each individual selectively attends to the people, objects and places that are of interest and importance to them. People rapidly adjust to their environment and select, organise and interpret information in a subjective way, which results in their particular understanding of reality.

We become accustomed to those stimuli that we are exposed to as a normal and routine part of our day-to-day lives, such as the tick of a watch, the background noise from a television or radio, the appearance of objects around our house. As stimuli become familiar we become used to the sensory experiences and they do not cross the perceptual threshold level. The fact that we become so used to some stimuli that we no longer notice them is called **habituation**. This process ensures that people can deal with the familiar and accommodate new information. Individuals become habituated to sensory information that they are familiar with and perceive information that is new, different, unusual and exceptional, which facilitates the process of learning. To some degree, *perception occurs by exception* and our attention is focused on people, objects or situations that are in some way different from our previous level of adaptation or habituation.

Factors that influence perception

A number of factors have been identified that influence the direction of our attention and therefore influence the process of perception. These factors relate to the individual, the object and the context.

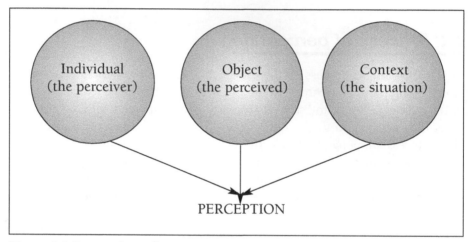

Figure 2.1 Factors that influence perception

- **Individual** – These factors relate to the individual, or the perceiver, and include interests, needs, motives and expectations. These internal factors contribute to the subjective nature of the process of perception. People select information that is relevant and meaningful to them.
- **Object** – This relates to the physical characteristics of the object that is perceived. These external characteristics cause people's attention to be drawn to a particular stimulus. The external factors relate to what is perceived and include contrast, intensity, size, movement, repetition and position.
- **Context** – Situational processes impact on the perceptions and the judgements that people form. These include *physical factors,* such as whether the environment is formal or informal and as a result is governed

by many or few rules and regulations that affect perceptions and behaviour; *social factors*, including the type of people in the environment and the person's relationship to and/or past experience of them; and *organisational factors* that provide an understanding of the nature of the company, such as the size of the organisation, its culture and its purpose.

The process of perception includes the following:

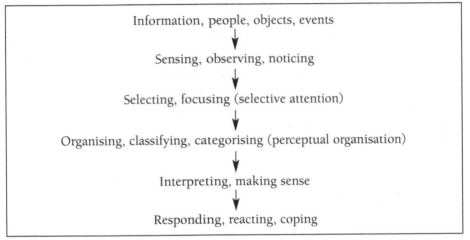

Figure 2.2 Stages in the perception process

2.3 Person perception and perceptual distortions

According to Arnold *et al.* (2005), **person perception** concerns how we obtain, store and recall information about other people to make judgements about them. Accurate perceptions help us to understand and to relate well with others, to get the best from them and to manage social situations with skill. Social perceptions are influenced by our perception of self.

Perceptual distortions/biases/errors

The subjective nature of the process of perception causes a number of distortions or biases to occur. It is important to understand these errors in order to increase awareness of these mistakes and to become a more accurate judge of others. Some sources of perceptual errors are examined below.

Stereotypes

A stereotype is a generalised belief about a person or group of people that may or may not accurately reflect reality. Stereotypes are developed when individuals are unable or unwilling to gather all of the information needed to make a fair judgement about people or situations. In the absence of the whole picture, stereotypes often allow people to fill in the gaps in their knowledge and understanding.

Stereotyping is the tendency to categorise or label people so that they can be placed in the perceiver's mind and characteristics can be attributed to them. *Stereotypes are generalised beliefs about characteristics, attributes and behaviours of members of certain groups* (Hilton and Von Hippel, 1996).

Stereotypes may be positive or negative, they may be accurate or inaccurate about the average characteristics of a particular group and can lead to discriminatory behaviour. Stereotypes can also have positive and negative social consequences. From a positive perspective, stereotypes allow individuals to make better informed judgements of other people about whom they have little or no personal information. In some circumstances, stereotyping may enable individuals to arrive at more accurate conclusions. A negative aspect of stereotyping is that, over time, those who are stereotyped negatively may display *self-fulfilling prophecy* behaviour. This results in the assumption by the individual that the stereotype represents a normal and accurate reflection of themselves, and may cause them to act out or imitate the associated behaviours.

Other negative effects of stereotyes include forming inaccurate opinions of people, scapegoating, erroneous judgements and reduced empathy. Stereotypes vary in favourability and extremity. Stereotypes do not allow exceptions since they assume that all the members of a particular group have the same characteristics. They are not always valid and can lead to an overestimation of differences. For example, all men cannot cook and all women are too sensitive for business.

Stereotypes generalise and simplify complex situations and involve the use of limited information. They can lead to the creation of negative views of people in other groups. They are resistant to change and tend to be used when people are under time pressure to make judgements and at low points in people's circadian rhythm, that is when they are tired. Also, people use stereotypes when their self-esteem and feelings of security are threatened. Stereotypes tend to make people feel superior in some way to the person or group being stereotyped.

Common stereotypes are based on:

- Age
- Ethnicity
- Gender
- Nationality
- Disability
- Profession

- Sexual orientation
- Race
- Religious belief
- Size
- Physical appearance
- Social class.

Society often innocently creates and perpetuates stereotypes, but these stereotypes can lead to unfair discrimination and persecution when the stereotype is unfavourable. Television, books, comic strips and movies provide an abundant source of stereotyped characters.

Projection

Psychological projection or projection bias is a defence mechanism that causes a person to unconsciously reject attributes about themselves that they believe to be unacceptable and to ascribe them to other people or objects in the world around them. It involves the projection of uncomfortable thoughts and/or feelings onto other people that they need to repress. Projection reduces the stress and anxiety that is associated with these thoughts and emotions by providing a means of expression for them. Developed by Sigmund Freud (1856–1939), this theory involves people attributing their own undesirable traits to others. For example, an employee might state that a colleague must be very jealous of the candidate chosen for promotion, but in reality they are expressing their feelings of jealousy. Projection facilitates the expression of unwanted, unconscious impulses or desires without permitting the conscious mind to acknowledge them.

In addition, projection may be used by individuals to obliterate attributes of other people that they are uncomfortable with. The individual assumes that the other person is like them and in so doing ignores the attributes they possess that make them feel uncomfortable. An example may involve a person making the assumption that because a person works on the same team as them that they must be working hard and that they are dedicated to the task at hand, as opposed to negatively regarding aspects of their performance.

Forms of projection include:

- **Neurotic projection** – This involves perceiving others as operating in ways that you unconsciously find objectionable in yourself.
- **Complementary projection** – This is based on the assumption that others do, think and feel in the same way as you.
- **Complimentary projection** – This relates to the belief that others can do things as well as you.

Finally, projection appears where people see their own traits in other people; this is called the *false consensus* effect. The result is that individuals sometimes see their friends as being more like them than they really are.

Projective techniques have been developed to assist the assessment of personality. Two examples are the Rorschach ink-blots and the Thematic Apperception Test.

The halo effect

This occurs when a single characteristic is used to generate an overall positive impression and, on the basis of this characteristic, other similar and logical characteristics are attributed to the individual. When a person is considered to be good (or bad) in one category, similar evaluations are likely to be made in other categories. The **halo effect** has been known since Edward Thorndike first named it in 1920.

The first traits that are recognised in other people influence the interpretation and perception of later traits as a result of expectations. For example, attractive people are often evaluated as having a more desirable personality and more skills than someone of average appearance. Also, the halo effect can be seen in practice when celebrities are used to endorse products, some of which they have no expertise in evaluating. In the process of selection, the interviewer may be influenced by candidates' positive attributes and ignore their weaknesses.

The opposite of the halo effect is called the *rusty halo* or the *horns, trident* or *devil effect*. This occurs when an individual is judged to have a single undesirable trait and is subsequently evaluated to have many poor traits. In this way, a single negative trait or weak point influences the perception of the person in general.

Implicit personality theories

Individuals have their own theories about which personality characteristics tend to go together, such as fat and jolly or hard-working and honest. People hold a particular belief about what a 'typical x' is like, and these expectations influence our perception of behaviour.

Implicit personality theories are general expectations that individuals construct about a person when they know something of their central traits. For example, happy people are believed to be friendly, intelligent people are assumed to be arrogant, aggressive people are stupid and quiet people are timid.

Attribution theory

The social psychology theory of attribution was developed by Fritz Heider in 1958. He suggested that people logically attempt to uncover connections between causes and effects. Attribution theory analyses the processes by which people infer the intentions and dispositions of others and explain events in terms of being caused by themselves or others.

Attribution theory examines how individuals interpret events and how this influences their thinking and behaviour. The theory focuses on the ways in which people explain (or attribute) the causes of the behaviour of others, or their own behaviour (self-attribution), by linking it to something else and explains how individuals 'attribute' causes to events.

According to Kelley (1967), people all act like naïve scientists in trying to understand the causes of behaviour. When judging the actions of others, the following three factors are examined:

- **Distinctiveness** – Does the person behave like this everywhere?
- **Consistency** – Does the person behave like this all the time?
- **Consensus** – Does the person behave like everyone else?

Through studying these factors, an attempt is made to establish a theory about the reasons for a person's behaviour and whether it is as a result of internal or external factors. *Internal, or dispositional, factors* relate to the person themselves and include intelligence, skill, ability and talent. *External, or situational, factors* relate to the environment and include chance, the situation and help from others.

Kelley observed that people tend to make a *fundamental attribution error.* When people are judging their own behaviour and a positive outcome results, they tend to attribute the causes to internal factors, but when the outcome is negative, they tend to attribute it to external factors. On the other hand, when judging others, it is the positive events that are attributed to external factors and the negative events to internal factors!

This error in perception suggests that feedback provided to employees in performance reviews may be predictably distorted by recipients depending on whether it is positive or negative.

Physical appearance

Judgements are quickly and often incorrectly made about individuals based on their physical appearance. Factors such as height, weight, age, facial symmetry, style of hair and dress, and level of perceived fitness influence judgements. Such physical qualities are used to attribute characteristics such as intelligence, honesty and health. These characteristics affect how we judge others, often without us being consciously aware of them.

Verbal communication

Information that people take into consideration includes an individual's accent, tone of voice and pitch. This provides an insight into geographical location, social background, educational level of achievement and even personality type.

Non-verbal communication

A lot of attention is paid to body language, including facial expressions, gestures and mannerisms. These provide a *sub-level of communication*. Non-verbal communication constitutes two-thirds of all communication (Hogan and Stubbs, 2003). It is more important in understanding human behaviour than words alone, as the non-verbal 'channels' appear to be more powerful than what people say. An incorrect message may be received if the body language used does not match the verbal message.

Ascribed attributes

These are beliefs that people hold about the type of attributes that are associated with those who have a particular status or are involved in a particular occupation. The higher the status of an individual, the greater the likelihood that they will be perceived to be self-assured and capable, such as the president of a country or the CEO of an organisation. Moreover, professionals such as doctors, lawyers and accountants may be deemed to be more important than others in the workplace. In both cases, people are not being judged on their own individual merits but as a result of the ascribed attributes.

First impressions

When people meet for the first time, it takes just a quick glance for a person to evaluate another individual. In this short time, one person forms an opinion about the other based on factors such as their appearance, body language and mannerisms.

The information that is initially received about another person has an enduring effect, as it triggers a person's *perceptual set*, which is an individual's predisposition to respond in a particular way, or a perceptual expectancy. Perceptual set has been shown to influence our evaluations of others in many social contexts. People who are told before they meet a person that this individual is 'warm' are more likely to perceive a variety of positive characteristics in them, as compared with when the word 'cold' is used in the description. It has been found that when an individual has a reputation for being funny, people are more likely to find them amusing. A person's perceptual set or perceptual expectancy reflects their personality traits. We often quickly identify our own traits in others. For example, people who are outgoing are quicker to identify traits of sociability in the behaviour of others.

Initial judgements are made that form the basis for the interpretation of subsequent behaviour. It is important for people both in their careers and social life to know how to make a good first impression.

Disposition and self-concept

A **disposition** relates to a person's mood, temperament, state of readiness or tendency to act in a particular way. The *mood* that an individual is in when judging others affects the information that they receive; is the glass half empty or half full?

In addition, the better the understanding and acceptance that individuals have of themselves, the more effective their judgement of others will be. **Self-concept,** or **self-identity,** is the knowledge and understanding that people have about themselves. It is the picture that people have of themselves and is closely connected to how a person behaves. A positive self-view will lead to a high level of self-esteem. A negative self-view will lead to lower levels of self-esteem and cause feelings of insecurity and a lack of self-confidence. The components of the self-concept include psychological, physical and social attributes, all of which are influenced by the individual's attitudes, habits, beliefs and ideas. A person's self-concept gradually becomes apparent in the early months of life and is shaped and reshaped due to life experiences.

Cognitive structure

Cognitive structures are patterns of physical or mental action that underlie particular acts of intelligence. Cognitive psychologists propose that a cognitive structure exists in each person's head. Cognitive structure may be understood as a large and delicately linked series of associations among words, concepts and whatever other mental entities exist. The more cognitively complex an individual is, the more accurate their understanding of others, as they are likely to perceive them based on multiple criteria.

2.4 General sources of errors and remedies in person perception

- Not collecting enough information.
- Using irrelevant or insignificant information.
- Individuals seeing only what they want and expect to see.
- Allowing early information to affect our perception.
- Permitting one's own characteristics to affect our judgements of others.
- Accepting cultural stereotypes uncritically.
- Attempting to decode non-verbal behaviour out of context.
- Basing attributions on flimsy and possibly irrelevant evidence. (Buchanan and Huczynski, 2010)

Methods to remedy errors in person perception

- Take time; avoid making hasty judgements about people.
- Collect and consciously use more information about people.
- Develop an enhanced self-awareness and insight into personal biases and preferences and how they affect judgements of others.
- Check attributions that are made about the causes of behaviour. (Buchanan and Huczynski, 2010)

2.5 Conclusion

The process of perception allows us to make sense of our world. Each person's perception of reality shapes the way they think, feel and behave. We perceive the world around us in different ways. Our perceptions of the world are influenced by many factors, including our personality, attitudes, values, motives, past experiences and expectations. Understanding our own perceptions and the perceptions of others will help us to explain our behaviour and the behaviour of others. Individuals see the world from their own perspective and can at times find it difficult to understand the way other people are thinking, feeling and behaving. Getting an insight into the reasons why people behave the way they do is critical to understanding their perception of the situation. This involves gaining information about the person, the people they are with and the environment that they are in. Then we can see the situation from the other person's perspective and make sense of their behaviour.

Managers need to have an understanding of how they perceive the world and make judgements about co-workers, employees, shareholders, customers, suppliers, regulators and others. The process of perception plays a central part in the selection and appraisal of employees, the willingness of co-workers to co-operate and the effective operation of teamwork. People are constantly managing the impression that they make on others. It is important to remember that other people may not perceive us in the way that we perceive ourselves or would like to be perceived. The reactions that individuals make to perceptions in the workplace include their levels of motivation, job satisfaction, commitment, absenteeism and turnover. Managers should constantly attempt to understand how employees perceive the workplace and the impact that has on performance. Finally, perception is of significant importance in the cultivation and management of an organisation's corporate image.

Summary

- Definition of perception.
- Process of perception.
- Biases in person perception.
- Methods to remedy errors in person perception.

Theory to real life

1. How does an insight into the process of perception help you to understand the world around you?
2. What biases/distortions/errors are you now aware of in how you perceive others?
3. Consider the biases in other people's perceptions and the influence that they have on their behaviour.
4. What factors may affect an employee's perception of their manager/boss?
5. Describe how positive and negative perceptions may influence the performance of employees.
6. How do the errors in social perception impact on the processes of selection and performance appraisal?
7. What advice would you give to people about overcoming their errors in judging others in the workplace?

Exercises

1. To demonstrate how people become used to the familiar and tend to pay most attention to new information, take out a blank page and, without looking, draw a picture of your watch face.
2. Discuss the stereotypes that you believe are held in society today and consider how these influence people's perception and behaviour.
3. Before making an important judgement or decision, take time to ask yourself a few key questions:
   - Am I motivated to see things a certain way?
   - What expectations do I have about the situation?
   - Would I see things differently without these motives and expectations?
   - Have I consulted with others who have the same motives and expectations?

By asking yourself these questions, you can start to examine many of the cognitive and motivational factors that cause bias in perception and influence decision-making.

4. Assumptions influence how we perceive and respond to people in our daily lives in the workplace. The purpose of this exercise is to help you to identify the assumptions that you have about other people. This task may be difficult as you are asked to identify and examine stereotypical assumptions that you may hold. It is important that you acknowledge and examine these beliefs as they affect how you think, feel and behave. An awareness of these assumptions can lead to changes in perceptions and behaviours.

Dimensions of diversity	Assumptions that might be made	Influence on behaviour in the workplace
Gender		
Educational background		
Work experience		
Appearance		
Physical ability		
Marital status		
Sexual orientation		
Religion		
Recreational habits		
Personal habits		

Essay questions

1. Propose a definition of perception and describe the process of perception.
2. Investigate the main sources of social bias in perception.
3. Outline the general sources of errors in person perception and how they may be overcome.

Short questions

1. Perception can be described as an active, dynamic, mental or_____ process.
2. Is it possible to avoid biases in perception?
3. Propose a definition of perception.
4. Each person has their own understanding of the world around them; therefore perception is a _____ process.
5. What process must occur before perception?
6. What is the name given to the boundary between sensing and not sensing?
7. What is the name given to the process by which we filter or screen out information that we do not need in order to prevent total bombardment of the senses?
8. Name the three overall factors that influence perception.
9. Identify three *internal* factors affecting perception.
10. Identify three *external* factors that cause us to notice environmental stimuli.
11. Name three characteristics of stereotypes.
12. When are we most likely to use stereotypes?
13. Provide two examples of workplace stereotypes.
14. What is projection?
15. When we use a single characteristic to generate an overall positive impression, this is aclled the _____ effect.
16. According to attribution theory, what are the three factors that we judge people on the basis of?
17. What do we attribute the causes of our success to, and to what do we attribute the causes of our failures?
18. Provide an example of one of your implicit personality theories.
19. Identify three sources of perceptual errors.
20. Name two remedies to perceptual errors.
21. Name two organisational applications of person perception.

3
ATTITUDES IN ORGANISATIONS

Objectives

This chapter will help you to:

- Define an attitude.
- Describe the structure and functions of an attitude.
- Examine the nature of cognitive dissonance.
- Explain the nature of job satisfaction.
- Recognise the factors leading to organisational commitment.

3.1 Employee attitudes defined

Employee attitudes have a significant impact on the success or failure of an organisation. Attitudes influence everything from customer service to employee turnover and profits. People's attitudes affect how they behave in the workplace.

An attitude is a method of expressing feelings. They are formed as a result of people's values, experiences and personalities. Individuals form attitudes about everything in the world around them, such as their family, friends, job, organisations, products and events. Attitudes have an impact on people in the workplace and affect performance, absenteeism and turnover.

Attitudes are developed as a result of our perceptions and are positive or negative. Since attitudes are acquired, they can be changed. Ultimately, they help people to make sense of the world around them.

According to Bird and Fisher (1986), an attitude is '**a person's relatively enduring disposition toward people, objects, events or activities**'.

Robbins *et al.* (2010) state that '**attitudes are evaluative statements – either favourable or unfavourable – about objects, people or events**'.

3.2 Attitude structure

An attitude is made up of three basic building blocks represented by the following three components:

1. **Belief** – The knowledge, beliefs, information and opinions that you have

about a particular person or job. The information you have may or may not be accurate, as it is based on perceptions of truth and reality. This is also called the *cognitive element* of an attitude.

2. **Feeling** – This refers to the emotional aspect of an attitude and concerns how you feel about something. This implies that you have evaluated the stimulus and like or dislike it. It is also termed the *evaluative, or affective,* aspect of an attitude.

3. **Action** – This is the aspect of an attitude that guides behaviour. It is made up of your predisposition, or intention, to behave in a particular way. However, this does not always result in actual behaviour; for example, the diet starts tomorrow! This is also called the *conative* component.

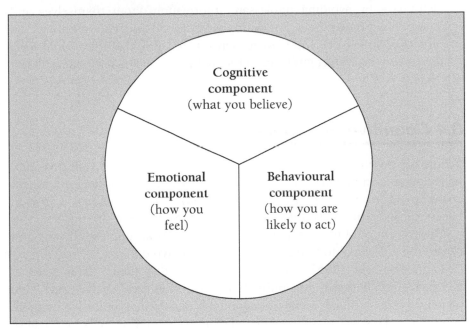

Figure 3.1 Elements of an attitude

3.3 Functions of attitudes

According to Katz (1960), attitudes have four important functions, or motivational bases, which collectively cause us to adopt a stable view of the world. Attitudes are held for the following psychological reasons:

1. **Knowledge function** – Attitudes give meaning to experience by helping people to organise their thoughts into coherent patterns. People mentally organise and structure the world so that it is understandable. This knowledge provides people with a *frame of reference*.

2. **Utilitarian function** – This is also called the *instrumental,* or *adjustive,* function. It enables people to categorise stimuli either positively or negatively. It directs individuals towards rewards and away from punishments, thereby explaining people's positive or negative attitudes. This function ensures that people get the most from social situations and achieve identified goals.
3. **Self-expressive function** – This function enables people to define and articulate the kind of people they are and to express the central values they hold. This function provides people with a self-identity.
4. **Ego-defensive function** – This allows people to project a positive self-image and to maintain their self-esteem. Individuals defend their self-image by avoiding unpleasant information about themselves and projecting it onto others. For example, your boss asks you to improve an aspect of your work and your response is to think that they could have given you the correct guidance in the first place, so it is not your fault but theirs!

3.4 Cognitive dissonance

People try to maintain consistency between the cognitive, affective and behavioural components of an attitude. Therefore, if one component changes, this causes feelings of inconsistency. For example, if a person believes that he or she is a good driver, but then fails the driving test, this produces feelings of tension and discomfort. This is an unpleasant state and causes the individual to find a way to remove or avoid it.

Leon Festinger (1957) described cognitive dissonance as a state of inconsistency between an individual's attitudes and behaviours. He contended that attitudes follow behaviour. A person may hold two or more conflicting ideas, beliefs or emotions. For example, individuals may realise that smoking is bad for their health but still continue to smoke. The feelings of discomfort, tension or cognitive upset experienced by the person causes them to reduce the tension by:

1. Changing the attitude.
2. Changing future behaviour.
3. Explaining or rationalising the inconsistency.

For example, Sophie is finding a co-worker unco-operative, unfriendly and very negative. Based on the concept of cognitive dissonance presented by Festinger (1957), she has three choices to reduce the tension or discomfort:

1. Sophie can change her attitude towards the co-worker by focusing on the person's positive traits and minimising their negative traits. This will enable Sophie to work more agreeably with her co-worker.
2. Sophie may deal with the situation by requesting a move to another team or department.
3. Another choice that Sophie has is to rationalise the situation. She may conclude that a part of work is learning to get along with people with a range of styles.

The creation of the experience of cognitive dissonance is frequently used as a marketing technique. This may involve providing people with an image of themselves today and what they could be like if they used a certain product (for example, toothpaste or cosmetics) in the future. Also, *attitudes change* initiatives are used in organisations that employ techniques of persuasion to create dissonance. During times of organisational change employees need to be made aware that current work practices or structures have to be altered. Therefore, employees need to think about changing their attitudes and behaviour in order to meet the changing requirements of the organisation. Cognitive dissonance demonstrates that attitudes influence behaviour, but also that behaviour can influence attitudes. People are motivated to reduce dissonance and act to regain mental harmony, thereby experiencing consonance.

3.5 Key work-related attitudes of job satisfaction and organisational commitment

Work-related attitudes are enduring beliefs, feelings and behavioural tendencies towards aspects of the job, the work environment and the people involved. Work-related attitudes are directly related to job performance, levels of absenteeism and turnover rates.

Job satisfaction

Job satisfaction concerns people's feelings or state of mind regarding the nature of their work. It can be influenced by a variety of factors, such as the quality of their relationship with their supervisor, the quality of the physical environment in which they work or the degree of fulfilment in their work.

Fundamentally, job satisfaction represents people's positive or negative feelings about their jobs. Employees develop attitudes to all the stimuli present in the workplace, including payment, benefits, promotional opportunities, the boss, co-workers and the canteen. In order to be satisfied, employees' expectations must be met; if they do not get what they expect, they become dissatisfied.

Job satisfaction has been defined by Locke (1976) as **'a pleasurable positive emotional state resulting from the appraisal of one's job or job-related experiences'**. It indicates the degree to which people find their work fulfilling and gratifying.

'Job satisfaction is the extent to which a person is gratified or fulfilled by his or her work' (Moorhead and Griffin, 2012).

The causes of job satisfaction have been identified by Hodgetts (1991) as:

- **Pay and benefits** – Is the level of payment adequate and fair and are the benefits flexible? Compensation represents management's view of the contribution made by the employee to the organisation. Pay has an intrinsic component as it is a reflection of an employee's efforts. It also has an extrinsic value in terms of the amount of payment received. Other rewards available to employees may include health insurance, pensions, childcare, company cars, allowances for lunches and membership of sports clubs.
- **Promotion** – Are there chances for further advancement? Is the system based on merit or seniority and how does this impact on job satisfaction?
- **The work itself** – Are the skills of the employees being used and enhanced? Is there clarity of role and is the work interesting and challenging? Are the person's expectations being met?
- **Leadership** – Is the leadership style task- or relationship-oriented and how appropriate is this style to the achievement of the goal?
- **Work group** – Is the work group friendly, co-operative and respectful of members? Do those in the work group provide support for each other?
- **Working conditions** – How safe and comfortable is the work environment?

The consequences of job satisfaction in the workplace include higher levels of performance and reduced employee absenteeism and turnover. In addition, satisfied employees experience better physical and mental health, learn more quickly, have fewer accidents, file fewer grievances and exhibit organisational citizenship behaviours.

Organ (1988) defines *organisational citizenship behaviour* (OCB) as '*individual behavior that is discretionary, not directly or explicitly recognized by the formal reward system, and that in the aggregate promotes the effective functioning of the organization*'. This definition highlights the fact that this type of behaviour results from personal choice and is not due to a job description, it goes beyond requirements and it makes a positive contribution to the organisation.

At the other end of the spectrum to OCB is *counterproductive work behaviour* (CWB). This type of behaviour goes against the goals of an organisation. According to Dalal (2005), *such behaviour is often related to feelings of job dissatisfaction and involves the employee purposely disrupting relationships, organisational culture or performance in the workplace.* CWB includes ineffective job performance, absenteeism, turnover, theft and accidents.

Job satisfaction can be promoted in the following ways (Greenberg and Baron, 2005):

- **Pay people fairly** – It is important that people believe that the organisation's pay system is fair with regard to hourly pay, salaries and fringe benefits.
- **Improve the quality of supervision** – Employees are most satisfied when they believe that their supervisors are competent and have respect for them and when there is open communication.
- **Decentralise the control of organisational power** – When people can participate freely in the process of decision-making, it creates feelings of satisfaction as they believe they have some impact on their organisation.
- **Match people to jobs that are in line with their interests** – People have a wide variety of interests and to ensure job satisfaction it is important that they are able to fulfil some of these in the workplace.

A lot of debate surrounds the relationship between job satisfaction and performance. The beliefs exist that job satisfaction enhances performance: 'a happy worker is a productive worker'; that high levels of performance cause job satisfaction; and that job satisfaction and performance are interdependent and are both affected by the availability of rewards (Schermerhorn *et al.*, 2011).

Organisational commitment

Organisational commitment is the relative strength of an individual's identification with and involvement in an organisation (Mowday *et al.*, 1982).

Schermerhorn *et al.* (2011) state that '**organizational commitment is the loyalty of an individual to an organization**'. Organisational commitment concerns a person's identification with and attachment to the organisation. Highly committed employees will perceive themselves as proud members of the organisation and express this by saying things such as 'we are proud of the quality of our customer service'. They will disregard minor causes of dissatisfaction and see themselves being part of the organisation into the future. The opposite is true of people with a low level of organisational commitment. When they talk about the organisation it may be in terms such as 'they don't value their employees around here'. They experience more sources of dissatisfaction and do not see themselves as part of the organisation into the future.

According to Griffin and Bateman (1986), organisational commitment has three components:

1. A desire to maintain membership.
2. A belief in and acceptance of the organisational values and goals and also an identification with the organisation.
3. A willingness to exert effort on behalf of the organisation.

Meyer and Allen (1991) developed a three-component model of commitment based on earlier research which indicated that there are three 'mindsets' that can characterise an employee's commitment to the organisation:

1. **Affective commitment** – This represents the employee's positive emotional attachment to the organisation. An employee who is affectively committed identifies strongly with the goals of the organisation and desires to remain a part of the organisation. This employee is committed to the organisation because he/she 'wants to' be.
2. **Continuance commitment** – The reason that the individual is committed to the organisation is because he/she perceives the high costs of losing organisational membership. These costs include financial (pay and benefits) and social (friendship and support) losses. The employee maintains their membership of the organisation because he/she 'has to'.
3. **Normative commitment** – Feelings of obligation cause the individual to be committed to and remain in the organisation. A number of factors may lead to the employee's feelings of obligation. The person may feel, for example, a 'moral' obligation to work hard and remain a member as the organisation may have invested resources in training and they feel they need to 'repay the debt'. In addition, intrinsically the person may believe strongly that people should be loyal to their organisation. The employee stays with the organisation because he/she 'ought to'.

According to Meyer and Allen, these three components of commitment are not mutually exclusive and an employee can therefore be simultaneously committed to the organisation in an affective, continuance and normative sense at varying levels of intensity. Based on this idea, Meyer and Herscovitch (2001) contend that at any point in time, an employee has a 'commitment profile' that reflects high or low levels of all three of these mindsets. Different profiles will have varying effects on workplace behaviour, including job performance, absenteeism and turnover.

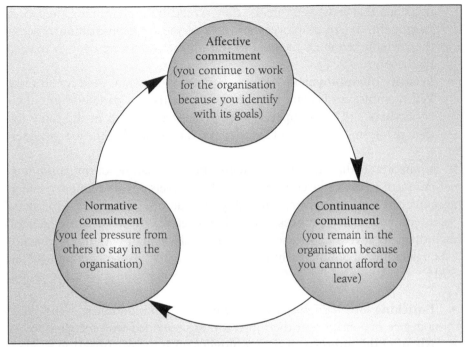

Figure 3.2 Meyer and Allen's (1991) three-component model of organisational commitment

Factors leading to organisational commitment include:

- **Intrinsic factors** – This relates to an individual's belief that if 'the organisation is good to me, I will be good to it'. Positive feelings can be created by providing employees with a greater sense of personal autonomy and more challenging assignments.
- **Person's nature** – Some people naturally have a predisposition to be committed to the organisation that they work for, and others do not.
- **Age** – Older employees may be more committed for a number of reasons, including the personal investment they have made in the organisation over the years, but also because it may be more difficult for them to get other employment with a similar status and remuneration.
- **Time spent in the organisation** – The longer an employee remains a member of an organisation, the more time and effort they have invested and they may be reluctant to leave it all behind. They will also have formed many important social bonds during that time.
- **Participation in decision-making** – When people are involved in making decisions that affect them in the workplace, they are usually very supportive of these being implemented. If they were to question the

decisions that have been made, they would be undermining their own judgement. When employees are part of the decision-making process, they usually remain a member of the organisation long enough to reap the benefits.

- **Security of employment** – People have a fundamental need for security. When employees become used to the demands of a particular job, their co-workers and their supervisor, it is easier to remain in the same job than risk losing the sense of security and familiarity that the job provides.

It is important that managers understand the nature of organisational commitment to avoid the consequences of low levels of commitment, such as absenteeism and turnover; unwillingness among employees to share resources and make sacrifices; and other negative personal consequences, including employees experiencing feelings of discontent with life in general.

Organisational commitment can be enhanced by (Greenberg and Baron, 1995):

- **Enriching jobs** – Employees are more likely to be committed if they have a degree of control over their jobs and are provided with recognition.
- **Aligning the interests of the employees with the organisation** – When both parties have the same interests in mind, the level of commitment is higher; this can be achieved by initiatives such as profit-sharing schemes.
- **Recruiting and selecting newcomers whose values closely match those of the organisation** – The closer the values of the individual to those of the organisation, the stronger the level of commitment. During the recruitment and selection process, it is important for both parties to gain an understanding of each other's values. These values are often documented in an organisation's mission statement.

3.6 Conclusion

Attitudes are complex and difficult to study. They are often inferred from the behaviour of individuals. Attitudes are held about people, objects, events and situations. People's attitudes reflect their experiences and reactions to particular stimuli. They have three components: cognitive, affective and behavioural. Attitudes have important functions: they allow people to organise and structure information; to obtain reward and avoid punishment; to defend their self-image; and to express their central values. Attitudes are relatively stable over time, but do change. The work-related attitudes of job satisfaction and organisational commitment affect organisational outcomes such as performance, absenteeism and turnover.

Summary

- Attitudes defined.
- Structure of attitudes.
- Function of attitudes.
- Cognitive dissonance.
- Work-related attitudes: job satisfaction, organisational commitment.

Theory to real life

1. How do your attitudes affect your behaviour in college and/or at work?
2. Consider your attitude to your OB course. What are your beliefs about the course? How positively or negatively do you feel about the course? How do you behave towards the course (through, for example, your attendance rate at lectures and tutorials, or time spent revising notes and reading textbooks)?
3. How satisfied are you with the job that you currently have (or one that you previously held)? What causes you to be satisfied and how does your level of satisfaction influence your behaviour?
4. Recall the organisation that employed you for the greatest length of time and identify the main reasons that you stayed working for that organisation.

Exercises

1. Within your class or tutorial group, identify examples of organisational citizenship behaviour and counterproductive work behaviour and consider their impact on an organisation.
2. Identify examples of times – in college, work and/or as a consumer – that your attitudes to stimuli (people, objects, events) changed due to the experience of cognitive dissonance.
3. Prepare a presentation to the owner/manager of a local business about the benefits of promoting job satisfaction and enhancing organisational commitment.

Essay questions

1. Propose a definition of an attitude and describe the structure of an attitude.
2. Examine the functions of an attitude, using examples.
3. Describe the nature of cognitive dissonance.
4. Explain the major causes and consequences of job satisfaction.
5. Describe the major causes and consequences of organisational commitment.

Short questions

1. Propose a definition of an attitude.
2. Name the three components/parts of an attitude.
3. Name the four functions of an attitude.
4. What is cognitive dissonance?
5. What three methods, according to Festinger (1957), can be used to reduce cognitive dissonance?
6. Identify four causes of job satisfaction.
7. What do the abbreviations OCB and CWB stand for?
8. What are three consequences of employees experiencing job satisfaction?
9. Name the three types of commitment, according to Meyer and Allen (1991).
10. Identify three factors influencing an individual's level of organisational commitment.
11. Name two consequences of low organisational commitment.
12. How can organisational commitment be enhanced?

4
LEARNING

Objectives

This chapter will help you to:

- Understand the nature of learning.
- Describe the behaviourist approach to learning.
- Explain the cognitive approach to learning.
- Identify social learning theory.
- Describe the structure of human memory.
- Apply methods of improving memory.

4.1 Learning defined

Learning occurs at all levels of the organisation – individual, group and the organisation itself. It is fundamental to the success of an organisation that an understanding is gained of how and why individuals learn and of how the organisation can facilitate continuous learning. Learning theories provide an insight into individual differences and management practices. This knowledge affects the design and delivery of induction and job training programmes, the design of reward systems and the provision of feedback to employees. It contributes to the successful management of organisational change and the creation of learning organisations.

According to Buchanan and Huczynski (2010), **'learning is the process of acquiring knowledge through experience which leads to a lasting change in behaviour'**.

Moorhead and Griffin (2012) state that learning can be defined as **'a relatively permanent change in behaviour or behavioural potential resulting from direct or indirect experience'**.

The main characteristics of learning include:

- **Learning involves change** – This may affect the way individuals think, feel and behave. People may or may not be aware of these changes.
- **Change may be positive or negative** – An example of a positive change would be learning to use a new piece of technology in the workplace. A negative change may involve developing a negative attitude towards a co-worker.

- **The effects of learning tend to be long-lasting** – Learning has an enduring influence on an individual's thoughts, emotions and actions.
- **Learning influences people's actual and potential behaviour** – When a new learning experience takes place, the effects may be demonstrated immediately through behaviour; examples of this are when a person touches a hot surface or when runners are told to 'go' at the start of a race. However, many learning experiences are stored away in memory to be recalled later and thus potential or future behaviour is affected by learning at an earlier time. An example of this is all of the information that is stored by students but not demonstrated until the time of an exam.
- **Learning results from direct and indirect experience** – Individuals learn much in life from first-hand experience and, as the saying goes, 'have been there and got the T-shirt'; this is *direct* experience. Learning also occurs through *indirect* experience, which includes listening to the experiences of others, reading books, watching television, going to the movies and accessing information on the internet. People learn indirectly through these media.

It is central to the ongoing success of an organisation that an environment is created within the workplace that regards learning, continuous development and improvement as the norm. These organisations will achieve competitive advantage, be innovative and effectively meet the changing needs of the environment.

4.2 Approaches to learning

A number of different approaches to explaining human learning exist. These include the **behaviourist approach,** the **cognitive approach** and **social learning theory**. Behaviourism is concerned primarily with the observable and measurable aspects of human behaviour. The cognitive approach examines the mental activities involved in learning. Social learning theory emphasises the importance of observing and modelling the behaviours, attitudes and emotional reactions of others as a means of learning.

4.3 The behaviourist approach

Behaviourism is primarily concerned with the observable and measurable aspects of human behaviour. This approach to learning originated from the work of American psychologist John B. Watson in 1913. He was critical of the introspective methods used by Sigmund Freud and others. According to

Watson, psychology was not concerned with the mind or with human consciousness, but only with the scientific examination of behaviour. Using scientific methods, the *causes and consequences* of behaviour could be clearly studied and identified. In this way, people could be studied in an objective manner like apes and rats.

Behaviourists assumed that the only things that are real are those things that can be seen and observed. The mind cannot be viewed directly, but how people act, react and behave can be seen. Inferences can be drawn from behaviour about the mind and the brain, but mental processes are not the primary focus of the investigation. The behaviour of individuals and not what they think or feel is the purpose of the study. Watson assumed that behaviour represents certain learned habits, and his studies attempted to determine how they were learned.

Behaviourism claims that psychology is the science of behaviour and not the science of the mind. Behaviour can also be described and explained without reference to internal mental states (such as memory), as the sources of behaviour are external (environment), not internal (mind). The behaviourists uphold the view that human beings are shaped through constant interaction with the environment.

The behaviourist approach asserts that mental processes are not directly observable and therefore are not valid issues for study. Its objective was to develop principles by which behaviour could be predicted and controlled. Learning is a function of experience. Ideas that are experienced together tend to be **associated** with each other. In addition, learning occurs through feedback from the environment, which can be rewarding or punishing. The primary focus of the approach is on the study of the visible stimulus and visible response, referred to as the **stimulus-response (S-R) link**. For this reason, it is also called the stimulus-response approach to learning.

Behaviourism has been criticised for not taking into account all kinds of learning; it disregards the activities of the mind and does not consider free will and internal influences, such as moods, thoughts and feelings. However, the behaviourist approach has made a significant contribution to understanding psychological functioning and has enhanced the credibility of psychology as a science. Using the principles of behaviourism, Pavlov and Skinner developed theories of learning.

Pavlovian/Classical conditioning

Russian psychologist Ivan Pavlov (1849–1936) discovered **classical conditioning**, which is based on stimulus-response relationships. In classical conditioning, learning occurs when a new stimulus begins to elicit behaviour similar to that originally produced by an old stimulus.

Pavlov studied animals' responses to conditioning. In his best-known experiment, Pavlov rang a bell when he was feeding some dogs their meals, which consisted of meat. Each time the dogs heard the bell, they knew a meal was coming and they would begin to salivate. Pavlov then rang the bell without bringing food, but the dogs still salivated. They had been 'conditioned' to salivate at the sound of a bell. Pavlov believed that humans react to stimuli in the same way.

Pavlov referred to the meat as an *unconditioned stimulus (UCS)* because it is one that unconditionally, naturally and automatically triggers a response. He called the salivating behaviour the *unconditioned response (UCR)* because it is an unlearned response that occurs naturally in response to the unconditioned stimulus.

The sound of the bell is termed the *conditioned stimulus (CS)*. It was a *neutral stimulus* until it became associated with the unconditioned stimulus (the meat) and after some time acted to trigger a *conditioned response (CR)*. After repeating this procedure a number of times, Pavlov was able to remove the UCS (the meat) and by only ringing the bell, the dogs would salivate (CR).

The dogs have now learned to respond to the sound of the bell by salivating, which was a previously neutral stimulus. The **association** between the meat and the sound of the bell had been established and the salivating behaviour is now called a conditioned response.

According to Pavlov, learning occurs when a conditioned response is linked to an unconditioned stimulus.

Table 4.1 Pavlov's theory of classical conditioning

Pavlovian conditioning proposes that the basic unit of learning is the conditioned response. Further changes in behaviour result from further conditioning.

Pavlov gathered much support for his theory of classical conditioning, but was not without his critics. Pavlovian conditioning:

*   Examines simple cause-and-effect relationships, but does not explain complex learning.
*   Ignores the concept of choice and makes the assumption that behaviour is reflexive or involuntary. However, individuals consciously and rationally make choices.

In reality, learning is a complex process and Pavlov's theory has its limitations. There are, however, numerous real-world applications for classical conditioning, such as in the treatment of phobias or anxiety problems and, in general, in the creation of an atmosphere in the workplace and classrooms that will enable people to perform effectively.

Skinnerian/Operant conditioning

American psychologist Bhurrus Frederick Skinner (1904–90) developed the theory of **operant conditioning,** or *instrumental conditioning*. Learning occurs through a method of rewards and punishments for behaviour. The theory proposes that an association is made between a behaviour and a consequence for that behaviour. Skinner denied that the mind or feelings play any part in determining behaviour; instead, he stated that an individual's experience of **reinforcements** determines their behaviour. The theory is based on the idea that behaviour is a function of its consequences and that learning is a function of change in overt behaviour. Changes in behaviour are due to a person's response to events (stimuli) that take place in the environment. Responses produce a consequence. When a particular stimulus-response (S-R) pattern is reinforced, the person is conditioned to respond. The distinctive feature of operant conditioning is that the organism can emit responses instead of only eliciting responses that are a result of an external stimulus.

Skinner was especially interested in the stimulus-response reactions of humans to various situations, and experimented with pigeons and rats to develop his theories. One of his best-known inventions is the *Skinner box*, which contains one or more levers that an animal can press, one or more stimulus lights and one or more places from which reinforcers, like food, can be delivered. In one experiment undertaken by Skinner, a starved rat was introduced into the box (or operant conditioning apparatus). When the rat pressed the lever, a small pellet of food dropped onto a tray. The rat soon learned that when it pressed the lever, it would receive a quantity of food. In this experiment, the rat's lever-pressing behaviour is reinforced by food.

Skinner also demonstrated that if pressing the lever is reinforced (by the rat getting food) when a light is on, but not when it is off, responses (pressing the lever behaviour) continue to be made in the light, but seldom, if at all, in the dark. The rat has learned to discriminate between light and dark. When the light is turned on a response occurs, but one that is different to a Pavlovian conditioned reflex response.

Through his experiments Skinner presented the ideas of *operant conditioning* and *shaping behaviour.* Shaping involves systematically reinforcing aspects of behaviour to achieve the desired results. Skinner applied his findings about animals to human behaviour.

Reinforcement is the central element in Skinner's theory. Reinforcement follows a specific response (stimulus-response-reinforcement). *Positive reinforcement* produces pleasant consequences and strengthens behaviour; it could involve the use of praise and recognition or feelings of increased accomplishment or satisfaction. It serves to maintain or increase the frequency of behaviour. *Negative reinforcement* involves the removal of an unfavourable event or outcome after the display of behaviour. Punishment is the presentation of an adverse event or outcome causing a decrease in the behaviour that it follows. This results in a decrease in behaviour, the avoidance of the aversive stimulus and can lead to the termination of behaviour.

Skinner paid particular attention to schedules of reinforcement and their influence on establishing and maintaining behaviour. The types of schedules of reinforcement consisted of *continuous*, *internal* (fixed or variable) and *ratio* (fixed or variable) schedules.

* **Continuous reinforcement** – This involves constant delivery of reinforcement for an action. Every time a specific action is undertaken, the subject instantly and always receives reinforcement. This method initially increases the frequency of behaviour but is prone to *extinction*. Extinction occurs when there is a breakdown in the association between the stimulus and response bond.
* **Interval (fixed/variable) reinforcement** – *Fixed interval reinforcement* is set for certain times. The subjects will quickly learn to discriminate between the times that they will receive reinforcement and when it is not available. For *variable interval reinforcement*, times between reinforcement are not set and frequently differ.
* **Ratio (fixed or variable) reinforcement** – *Fixed ratio reinforcement* deals with a set amount of work that needs to be completed before there is reinforcement. *Variable ratio reinforcement* involves a different amount of work (from the last amount of work) being needed to receive the reinforcement.

In a survey conducted by the *Review of General Psychology* in July 2002, Skinner was listed as the most influential psychologist of the twentieth century. Operant conditioning has been widely applied in clinical settings as well as in teaching and instructional development.

Classical conditioning approach to learning	Operant conditioning approach to learning
Unconscious	Conscious
Involuntary	Voluntary
Passive	Active
Responses drawn from subject	Responses made by subject
Reinforcement not influenced by responses	Reinforcement influenced by responses

Table 4.2 Classical vs. operant approaches to learning

Evaluation of behaviourist approach

Although the contribution that the behaviourist model has made has been widely accepted, the approach is not without its criticisms, which include:

- Ignoring the human ability to learn and engage in independent and complex thinking.
- Not considering the influence of the learner with regard to variables such as attitudes, emotions and level of motivation.
- Lack of attention to individual differences such as perceptions, attitudes, motivations, past experiences and expectations.
- Learning will cease in the absence of reinforcement.

The behaviourist approach to learning examined observable, reflexive responses. The challenge of the subsequent approach was to examine the mental or cognitive processes that affect learning and to understand what happens inside the head of the learner.

4.4 The cognitive approach

The **cognitive approach** to learning is also called the *information processing approach*. It attempts to examine the cognitive, or mental, structures influencing learning. Cognition refers to mental activities, including thinking, remembering, learning and language use. The theorists who advocate this approach believe that mental processes are important and are amenable to study. Their proposition is that learning involves more than simple stimulus-response (S-R) links and that cognitive factors play a central role in learning. They believe that consideration should be given to the internal workings of the mind and that people are conscious and active participants in how and what they learn.

According to cognitive theorists, people learn by drawing on their experiences, making choices about their behaviour and by acknowledging the consequences of their choices. Finally, they evaluate the consequences of their choices and add them to their experiences; this influences their future choices.

Two theorists who contributed to the cognitive approach to learning are Kohler and Tolman.

Insight learning

The German psychologist Wolfgang Kohler (1887–1967) was working at a primate research facility in the Canary Islands when the First World War broke out. While Kohler was marooned there, he had available to him a large outdoor pen and nine chimpanzees of various ages. Described by Kohler as a playground, the pen contained a range of objects including boxes, poles and sticks with which the primates could experiment.

Kohler undertook a number of problem-solving experiments with the chimpanzees, each of which involved obtaining food that was not directly accessible. Examples of these experiments are the *stick* and *box problems*.

In the *stick problem* one of the chimpanzees, called Sultan, learned to use bamboo sticks to retrieve bananas from outside his cage. The chimpanzee spent some time examining the elements of the problem, which consisted of the bananas and the sticks. As if in a sudden flash of inspiration, he inserted one stick into the other and constructed a pole that was long enough to pull the bananas into the cage. This problem was not solved by trial and error, but by a type of sudden inspiration or insight.

Another example of this type of learning is the *box problem*. Food was hung from the top of the pen, and a number of different solutions were used by the chimpanzees to solve Kohler's food-gathering puzzles. One chimp attempted to shin up a toppling pole it had placed underneath the bananas; several others succeeded by stacking crates underneath but found it difficult to get their centre of gravity right. Another chimp moved a crate under the bananas and used a pole to knock them down. It appeared to Kohler as if the chimps were solving the problem by a kind of cognitive trial and error, as if they were experimenting in their minds before manipulating the tools. The pattern of these behaviours – failure, pause, looking at the potential tools, and then the attempt – appeared to involve insight and planning.

Based on these experiments, Kohler identified the concept of **insight learning.** This type of learning or problem-solving involves the subject grasping the inner relationship between the elements of a problem. This perceived relationship is essential to arriving at the solution to the problem. Kohler's theory proposed that learning could occur by 'sudden comprehension' as opposed to gradual understanding. This is not trial-and-error learning. The experience of insight learning has also been referred to as the *'eureka experience'* and the *'aha moment'*.

Latent learning

Edward Chace Tolman (1886–1959), an American psychologist, has made several significant contributions to the field of psychology in general and in particular to studies of learning. While at the University of California-Berkeley, he developed a cognitive theory of learning. He believed that learning developed from pieces of knowledge and cognition about the environment and how the organism relates to it. This was in contrast to earlier theorists who proposed that learning was due to stimulus-response connections.

To study learning, Tolman undertook a number of classical rat experiments. One of his best-known studies, undertaken in 1938, investigated the role of reinforcement in the way that rats learn their way through complex mazes. These experiments eventually led to the theory of **latent learning,** which describes learning that occurs in the absence of an obvious reward.

Tolman put three groups of rats in a maze and observed their behaviour over a two-week period.

- **Group 1:** The rats in this group received a food reward every time they reached the end of the maze in a timely manner; they would not go down to the dead-end parts of the maze.
- **Group 2:** In this group, the rats did not receive a food reward and appeared to follow no particular path, as if they were just wandering around.
- **Group 3:** For the first ten days of the experiment, the rats in Group 3 seemed to wander around like the rats in Group 2 and found no food. On the eleventh day, Tolman placed food in the maze and from their response, it appeared that they had learned to go to the end of the maze without any reinforcement but did not want to. On day 12, the rats from Group 3 were performing as well as the rats from Group 1, which had been rewarded with food from the very beginning of the test. It appears that the rats from Group 3 used latent learning, since they did not immediately display the same performance as the rats in Group 1.

Latent learning takes place without an obvious source of reinforcement. In

Tolman's experiment, Group 3 did not receive any food until the eleventh day. They appeared to display characteristics demonstrating that they had acquired a 'mental image of the maze'. This shows that they had been learning during the first ten days, but without rewards the rats had no reason to act on what they had learned. Once they began to find the food, they went through the maze quickly.

This theory proposes that knowledge acquired with latent learning does not provoke a specific response but it does lead to knowledge about the consequences of a certain response. The rats learned how the maze was organised and understood which path would lead to a dead end and which path would lead to food. The acquisition of knowledge in this manner allows people to be flexible and creative in attaining their goals.

Latent learning occurs when the brain acquires knowledge at a particular date or time, without reinforcement, but does not use it until a later time when that knowledge is required. An example of this could be learning song lyrics and answers to trivia questions without realising it but being able to bring them to mind later when required.

Evaluation of the cognitive approach

According to the cognitive theorists, learning is influenced by individual factors such as perception, attitudes, motivation, feedback and memory. People do not just respond to stimuli, they organise and make sense of the information received.

4.5 Social learning theory

Canadian psychologist Albert Bandura's (1977) major premise was that people can learn by observing others. His social learning theory emphasises the importance of observing and modelling the behaviours, attitudes and emotional reactions of other people. Human behaviour is explained in terms of continuous reciprocal interaction between cognitive, behavioural and environmental influences. The component processes underlying observational learning are:

- **Attention** – The individual notices something in the environment.
- **Retention** – The individual remembers what was noticed.
- **Reproduction** – The individual produces an action that is a copy of what was noticed.
- **Motivation** – The environment delivers a consequence that changes the probability the behaviour will be emitted again (reinforcement and punishment).

Due to the fact that social learning theory includes attention, memory and motivation, it spans both cognitive and behavioural frameworks. Bandura believes that mind, behaviour and the environment all play a central role in the learning process. Social learning theory is also referred to as *observational learning* and *modelling.*

Social learning theorists believe that leaning is affected by an individual's '*self-efficacy*'. This refers to a person's evaluation about whether or not they can successfully acquire new knowledge and skills. Individuals high in self-efficacy are more likely to persevere and perform more effectively without becoming stressed than those with low self-efficacy (Gist and Mitchell, 1992). Research has demonstrated a significant relationship between high self-efficacy and high work performance.

4.6 Memory

Memory is an information-processing system that facilitates the retention and retrieval of information. Firstly, information is received from the senses; secondly, it is stored in memory; and thirdly, it is recovered from storage. Memory is an active cognitive system that acts to bridge the past and present.

According to Atkinson and Shiffrin (1968), there are three types of memory:

- Sensory memory
- Short-term memory
- Long-term memory.

The structure of memory

Sensory memory

The **sensory memory** receives information from the senses. An exact copy of sensory information is held in the sensory memory to permit its transfer to the short-term memory. A sensory memory exists for each sensory channel. For example, visual stimuli are held in the *iconic memory* for half a second, and aural stimuli are held in the *echoic memory* for two seconds. Information is passed from sensory memory into short-term memory by attention, therefore stimuli are filtered and only those that are of interest at a given time are transferred to the next memory system.

Short-term memory

The **short-term memory (STM)**, or active memory, allows the recall of information which is being processed at that point in time. It involves remembering and processing information at the same time. The STM holds information for a short period of time, typically twenty to thirty seconds. An example of STM is that in order to understand this sentence you need to retain in your memory the beginning of the sentence as you read to the end.

Short-term memory decays rapidly and has a limited capacity. Decay occurs in STM within fifteen to thirty seconds. Miller (1956) discovered that *chunking of information* could lead to an increase in the short-term memory capacity. Chunks are meaningful units of information such as letters, digits, words or phrases. Miller believed that the capacity of the STM was limited to seven chunks of information plus or minus two. A person with an average STM capacity will be able to recall seven chunks of information; if the storage space is less, only five or six chunks may be retained, but if the STM is used effectively, up to nine chunks of information may be stored.

In the STM, new information can be received only by replacing old information. Interference or interruption cause disturbance in STM retention that accounts for the need to complete the tasks held in short-term memory as soon as possible. Examples of the STM in action involve retaining a piece of information temporarily in order to complete a task, such as remembering an important point until another person finishes talking, or carrying over a number in a subtraction sum. The STM does not hold complete concepts but retains links and pointers, such as words, which the brain integrates with other accumulated knowledge. Information will quickly disappear or decay forever unless a conscious effort is made to retain it. Information that is important and valuable can be transferred to the next storage system through *rehearsal*. This involves active, conscious interaction with incoming information and may involve silent, inner speech.

Long-term memory

Information stored in the **long-term memory (LTM)** is based on meaning; meaningless information is therefore very difficult to commit to memory and to recall. The LTM is a relatively permanent storehouse of information and has a nearly limitless capacity. It is passive and therefore does not alter information. As the LTM is organised according to meaning, appropriate retrieval cues are needed to recover information. Poor memory results from retrieval failure. When information is recalled, it is transferred from the LTM into the STM. The STM is the active part of the memory and allows the combination of past and present experiences.

The LTM consists of two types of memory: *episodic memory* and *semantic memory*. Episodic memory represents memory for events and experiences in a serial form and therefore it is from the episodic memory that people can reconstruct actual events that have taken place at a given point in their lives. Semantic memory is a structured record of facts, concepts and skills that individuals have acquired.

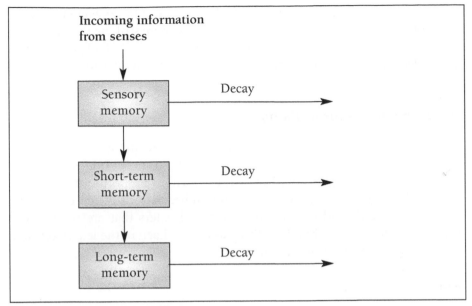

Figure 4.1 The structure of human memory

4.7 Mnemonic devices

Mnemonic devices are methods that can be used to give information meaning and aid memory.

Method of loci

This mnemonic device dates back to ancient Greek times and was used by Greek orators (speakers) to help them memorise speeches. To use the **method of loci**, think of a familiar building or journey, such as your house, or the drive or walk to college or work. Then take a mental walk along the route, for example through the rooms in your house, paying attention to well-defined parts of the rooms that make your mental images more vivid – these are the *loci*. A *locus* can be something like a door, a picture or a landmark. Ensure that you can travel in your mind easily from locus to locus as you visit your house or travel on your journey.

When you have identified your place and locations (for example, your house, your kitchen which contains the kettle, toaster, fridge and other loci), identify a list of words that you want to remember and associate each word with one of your locations. To recall the words and place them in the correct order, take a mental walk through your house, asking yourself questions such as what is in the kitchen, sitting room and other rooms. To be able to retrieve all of the items from memory, you should follow an order in your mental journey. When you associate the words that you need to remember with the loci, some surprising images will be created. The more striking the image, the more easily you will remember the items. For example, think of your kitchen where Pavlov is at the oven making dinner. On the floor beside him is his dog, in the fridge is a piece of meat and on the table is a bell!

Acronyms and abbreviations

Acronyms are shortened versions of names, using the initial letters of words or phrases pronounced as words; examples of these are NATO, laser and the famous Swedish furniture company IKEA, which is the short form for Ingvar Kamprad Elmtaryd Agunnaryd. Sometimes **abbreviations** are used, omitting the ends of words and leaving only the initial letters that are pronounced separately, such as IBM, FBI, UN, RSVP and ETA. Each of the letters acts as a cue to retrieve information from memory.

Acrostics

An **acrostic** is a poem or other writing in which the first letter, syllable or word of each line, paragraph or other recurring feature in the text spells out another new word or sentence. An acrostic can be used as a mnemonic device to aid memory retrieval.

Planets in order from the sun:

M y	Mercury
V ery	Venus
E ducated	Earth
M other	Mars
J ust	Jupiter
S ent	Saturn
U s	Uranus
N achos	Neptune

Colours of the rainbow:

R ichard	Red
O f	Orange
Y ork	Yellow
G ave	Green
B attle	Blue
I n	Indigo
V ain	Violet

The seven wonders of the ancient world:

S eems	Statue of Zeus at Olympia
L ike	Lighthouse of Alexandria
M atahari	Mausoleum at Halicarnassus
P icked	Pyramid of Giza
H er	Hanging Gardens of Babylon
T argets	Temple of Artemis at Ephesus
C arefully	Colossus of Rhodes

Methods of improving memory

- Break information down into small units or chunks of information.
- Give information meaning.
- Use imagery.
- Regularly rehearse information.
- Use mnemonic devices to aid memory.

4.8 Conclusion

Learning is a natural human ability that enables us to survive, adapt and develop within a wide range of environments. Learning and memory are vital processes in everyday life. The theories of learning provide a framework for understanding learning. Individuals differ in their learning style and capabilities. On both individual and organisational levels, learning involves the process of change. Organisations need to ensure that they can cope with the ever-changing turbulent environment. The role of learning is central to organisations in achieving their current strategies. In addition, continuous learning is vital for the future development of organisations.

Summary

- Learning defined.
- Theories of learning:
    - Behaviourist approach
    - Cognitive approach
    - Social learning theory.
- Memory.

Theory to real life

1. Think about the knowledge that you have acquired through association (advertisements contain many good examples).
2. How has your behaviour been shaped in school, college and/or work by reinforcement?
3. Consider your approach to solving complex problems in your daily life.
4. Think of examples of behaviour that people have learned through social learning.
5. How is an understanding of learning useful to managers and employees in organisations?
6. Think about the memory aids that you use when trying to remember information when making presentations or doing exams. What other methods could you use to improve your memory?

Exercises

1. Identify the aspects of the theories of learning that provide you with an insight into how you learn.
2. Using the method of loci, visualise a room and in a location in the room place each item to be memorised. In your mind, pick up each item as you take a mental walk around that room. Now try to list in order the items that you have attempted to store in your memory.
3. Look at a list or a sentence that you need to remember and write down in order the first letter of each word. Use these letters to form an acrostic that you can easily recall to ensure you remember the items on the list.

Essay questions

1. a. Propose a definition of learning.
   b. Investigate the reasons why the behaviourist approach to learning is often referred to as the stimulus-response approach.
2. Explain what is meant by insight and latent learning and how these theories contribute to our understanding of human learning.
3. Compare and contrast the behaviourist and cognitive approaches to learning. How have these theoretical approaches helped to provide an understanding of human learning?
4. Examine the differences between the behaviourist, cognitive and social learning theories.

5. Discuss the view that no single theory can adequately explain how human learning takes place.
6. Examine the structure of human memory and identify methods of improving memory.

Short questions

1. Learning involves _____, which affects the way individuals think, feel and behave.
2. The effects of learning are long lasting. TRUE/FALSE?
3. What is the aim of the behaviourist approach to learning?
4. What is the aim of the cognitive approach to learning?
5. According to the behaviourist approach to learning, ideas that are experienced together tend to be _____ with each other.
6. The behaviourist approach is also called the S-R approach. What do the letters S and R stand for?
7. What is another word for learning?
8. What learning theorist stated that the basic unit of learning was the conditioned response?
9. Skinner stated that behaviours that are rewarded tend to be _____.
10. _____ results in avoidance or the termination of behaviour.
11. Name two cognitive factors that influence the process of learning.
12. According to the cognitive approach, people are conscious and active participants in how and what they learn. TRUE/FALSE?
13. What is insight learning?
14. What is the name given to the type of learning that is not demonstrated by behaviour at the time of learning?
15. How do we learn, according to social learning theory?
16. Name the three types of memory.
17. Which part of memory is the working memory?
18. Name two mnemonic devices.
19. Identify two methods of improving your memory.

5
PERSONALITY

Objectives

This chapter will help you to:

- Propose a definition of personality.
- Describe the sources of personality.
- Explain the Big Five factors in personality that describe the differences between people.
- Appreciate the challenge of personality assessment.

5.1 Personality defined

Personality is an important factor in shaping behaviour. It is made up of a stable set of characteristics that can be used to make generalised predictions. In addition, personality traits can be used to assess and understand the differences between people.

According to Kagan and Havemann (1976), an individual's personality is **'the total pattern of characteristic ways of thinking, feeling and behaving that constitute the individual's distinctive method of relating to the environment'**.

Gross (1992) proposes that personality can be defined as **'those relatively enduring aspects of individuals which distinguish them from other people, making them unique, but which at the same time permit comparison between individuals'**.

Robbins *et al.* (2010) state that personality can be defined as **'the sum total of ways in which an individual reacts and interacts with others'**.

The definitions of personality highlight that individuals differ in how they think, feel and act and that personality causes people to behave relatively consistently over time and in different life situations. This consistency in turn leads to an insight into personality traits that characterise a person's regular way of responding to the environment around them.

Organisational problems are often attributed to personality flaws, personality clashes and personality conflicts. Managers require an understanding of personality in order to appreciate each person's style and its impact on job performance.

5.2 Where does personality come from?

The *nature versus nurture* debate explores the origins and development of personality. The debate concerns the relative importance of individuals' innate, genetic inheritance versus their life experiences. The research in this area focuses on the impact of nature and nurture in the development of individual differences.

Personality is affected by factors such as genetic inheritance, family experiences, culture and life experiences.

Genetic inheritance

Our genetic inheritance provides the genetic blueprint that determines personal characteristics such as intelligence, creativity and aggression. In addition, our gender impacts on our personality development.

Family experiences

Parents, siblings and family life shape the development of personality. Through family experiences, people are *socialised* and learn how to adapt to the environment around them. Parents have a significant impact on children and act as role models.

Alfred Adler (1870–1937), an Austrian psychiatrist, was one of the first theorists to suggest that birth order affects personality. He proposed that birth order can have a significant impact on an individual's style of life, which is a habitual way of dealing with the tasks of friendship, love and work. The position that a person has in the family as first, middle, last or only child plays a part in shaping personality.

According to Leman (2001), personality is influenced by position in the family.

First-borns	
Positives	*Negatives*
Natural leaders	Moody
High achievers	Insensitive
High level of control	'Know-it-alls'
Pay close attention to detail	Poor at delegating
Punctual	Perfectionists
Organised	
Competent	

⟶

Middle-borns	
Positives	*Negatives*
People pleasers Calm Down-to-earth Great listeners Good mediators and negotiators	Try to please everyone Not good at handling conflict Poor decision-makers
Last-borns	
Positives	*Negatives*
Strong people skills Make friends easily Extroverted Risk-takers	Fear of being rejected Short attention span Self-centred
Only children	
Positives	*Negatives*
Task-oriented Conscientious Dependable Like responsibility	Very demanding Don't accept criticism well Oversensitive

Table 5.1 How personality is influenced by position in the family (Leman, 2001)

Culture

Culture is patterns of beliefs, values and motives that are learned. Cultural norms create a predisposition to behave in a particular way by specifying ranges of tolerable behaviour.

Life experiences

The 'non-shared environment' of the family is a central factor in the attempt to gain an insight into the range of influences on personality development.

5.3 The Big Five

Psychologists have identified five dimensions that describe the distinct differences in personality between people.

1. Emotional stability

This characteristic relates to a person's ability to cope with stress and manage anxiety in their lives. Emotional stability represents the ability to respond in reasonable and consistent ways to challenges.

A person is rated along this dimension from emotionally stable to neurotic. The concept of neurotic anxiety was first identified by Sigmund Freud (1856–1939) and describes the struggle between internal impulses to act in a desired manner and pressure to be socially acceptable.

Those who are emotionally stable are less reactive to stress and are calm, even-tempered and feel less tense. The following characteristics are associated with **emotional stability:**

- Self-confident
- Adjusted
- Optimistic
- Resistant to irrational fears
- Easy-going
- Realistic
- Good at solving own problems
- Few health worries
- Few regrets.

Neuroticism lies at the other end of the dimension and can be defined as an enduring tendency to experience negative emotional states. Those who score high on neuroticism do not respond well to environmental stress and are more likely to interpret everyday situations as threatening and small sources of frustration as hopelessly difficult. Traits possessed by **neurotics** include:

- Unstable
- Anxious and easily upset
- Emotional
- Low self-esteem
- Feeling of disappointment with life
- Feeling of failure
- Pessimistic
- Depressed
- Worry about things that may never happen
- Obsessive
- Conscientious and highly disciplined
- Troubled by conscience
- Suffer from hypochondriasis.

2. Extroversion

A central dimension of human personality is **extroversion to introversion.** Extroverts (in some cases spelled 'extraverts') are assertive and seek out excitement. Introverts are reserved and are less likely to thrive on making new social contacts.

Carl Jung (1875–1961) popularised the terms 'extroversion' and 'introversion' and almost all comprehensive models of personality include the trait. Examples include Eysenck's Three-Factor model, the Myers-Briggs Type Indicator and the Big Five personality traits.

Extroverts are characterised by the fact that they direct their energies outwards to other people's actions and reactions. They tend to 'fade' when alone and get bored without other people around them. Extroverts are:

- Sociable
- Crave excitement
- Need to talk to people
- Optimistic and carefree
- Risk-takers, impulsive
- Like change

- Active
- Display emotion
- Tough-minded
- Aggressive
- Quick-tempered
- Unreliable.

Extroverts experience difficulties when working alone, reflecting on key issues, undertaking preparation, thinking before acting and concentrating on a single task.

Introverts direct their energies inwards to their own thoughts, feelings and ideas. They enjoy spending time alone and experience less reward in time spent with large groups of people. Introverts tend to concentrate on a single activity at a time and to observe situations before taking part in them. They tend to 'fade' when with others and can become overstimulated with too many other people around. Introverts are:

- Quiet, introspective, retiring
- Withdrawn, reserved
- Tender-minded
- Suppress emotions
- Effective planners

- Pessimistic
- Reliable
- Distrust impulse
- Appreciate order.

Introverts experience difficulties when working in large groups, articulating their thoughts and interacting with others.

3. Openness to experience

Through research, Rogers (1961) uncovered differences in people's degree of **openness to experience.** He believed that in order to be 'fully functioning', a person should be open to feelings and experiences. Those who are open are effective at incorporating new experiences into their understanding of the world. As a result, individuals who are open to experience have enhanced interactions with others, are good communicators and adapt well to change in their lives. According to Costa and McCrae (1992), openness involves active imagination, attention to inner feelings, preference for variety and intellectual curiosity. Those who are rated low on openness are considered closed to experience. They tend to be conventional and traditional and prefer familiar routines rather than new experiences and may be thought of as practical and down-to-earth. People who are open to experience are not any healthier or better adjusted than those who are closed to experience; these are just two different ways of relating to the world.

4. Agreeableness

This is a tendency to be pleasant and accommodating in social situations and to get along with others. Those who are agreeable are empathetic, considerate, friendly, generous, helpful and likeable. Agreeable people are optimistic and tend to believe that most people are honest, decent and trustworthy. These characteristics facilitate the development of satisfactory, easy and pleasant working relationships. This trait enables the person to build effective networks and enhances their performance at work. Those who have a high degree of agreeableness develop trusting relationships (Tobin *et al.*, 2000). Individuals who rate low on agreeableness place self-interest above getting on with others. As a result, they are less concerned with others' well-being and less likely to go out of their way to help others in general (Graziano *et al.*, 2007). They can be suspicious and unfriendly due to their scepticism and are more likely to compete than co-operate, whereas agreeable people tend to be concerned about others, and are co-operative and trusting.

5. Conscientiousness

Those who are conscientious demonstrate effective job performance in a wide range of environments. The characteristics that they possess include a high level of competence, order, duty, achievement orientation and self-discipline. Conscientious people are hard-working and reliable in general and, when this is taken to an extreme, may be perfectionists, compulsive in their behaviour and workaholics. Those who are low on conscientiousness tend to be more laid back, less goal-oriented and less driven by success.

The approach to personality presented by the Big Five model gives consideration mainly to the genetic influence on personality. However, it is important that situational influences are taken into account. The characteristics presented are generally believed to be universal, stable and enduring, but may be affected by life experiences and are subject to change. However, it is believed that some personality dimensions are more stable than others. The dimension of extroversion–introversion has been found to be relatively stable from childhood to adulthood. Whereas, the stability of the trait of conscientiousness may be influenced by the situation. Extraversion and conscientiousness are good predictors of successful performance in the workplace, according to Barrick and Mount (1993).

The Big Five traits can be used by managers to understand why employees behave the way they do and to make predictions about the most suitable person for a particular role. There is no 'one best type of personality', some people are suited to some types of jobs and organisations and organisations need to appreciate the value of diversity.

The Big Five factors can be remembered by the acronym OCEAN.

OPENNESS	Artistically sensitive, reflective, insightful, imaginative, curious
CONSCIENTIOUSNESS	Organised, efficient, reliable, self-disciplined, dutiful, ethical
EXTROVERSION	Outgoing, sociable, adventurous, assertive, active, gregarious
AGREEABLENESS	Trusting, gentle, warm, co-operative, tender-minded, non-critical
NEUROTICISM	Anxious, hostile, self-consciousness, emotionally unstable, vulnerable, impulsive

Table 5.2 The Big Five factors (Bernstein *et al.*, 2000)

5.4 Other personality-related characteristics

Behaviour in the workplace is also linked to the personality-related characteristics of locus of control, self-esteem and authoritarianism.

1. **Locus of control** – Individuals either have an *internal* or an *external locus of control*. Those with an internal locus of control believe that what happens to them is caused by them. Those with an external locus of control attribute what happens to them as being caused by factors outside of them.

   People who have an internal locus of control believe that they are masters of their own destiny and that their actions will have a direct effect on what happens to them. Those with an internal locus of control make their own decisions. In addition, they are more likely to be politically and socially active as they believe they can influence the shape of events.

   Those who have an external locus of control do not feel that they have much influence on what happens to them and that events will take place independently of their actions. Individuals who have an external locus of control prefer others to direct activities and make decisions for them.

2. **Self-esteem** – This refers to a person's evaluation of their self-worth and has a significant influence on behaviour. Those with a high self-esteem are independent, assertive, creative and risk-takers. They develop

effective relationships, but are not easily influenced by others. They set challenging goals for themselves and are not concerned about what others will think of them.

People with a low self-esteem look for the approval of others and are less confident. They take few risks, set easier goals and are critical of themselves. Self-esteem is related to an individual's overall sense of psychological well-being.

3. **Authoritarianism** – This describes a person's sensitivity to status, formal authority and official rules. Those with an 'authoritarian personality' tend to submit to higher status and are aggressive to those of a lower status. Allinson (1990) describes this as the 'bureaucratic personality', one that is driven by a fear of failure, prefers highly structured organisations and favours clear lines of authority and responsibility. Those who are authoritarian do not like to be given new tasks and resist change.

5.5 Personality assessment

The nature of personality presents difficulties in measurement and assessment. Methods used to assess personality and predict work behaviour include interviews, inventories (self-completed questionnaires), behaviour assessments, personality tests and e-assessment (on-line personality tests). To achieve reliable results, personality tests should be used in conjunction with methods such as interviews and aptitude tests.

The assessment of personality has a number of benefits:

- Psychological tests form a useful basis for recruitment, selection and promotion decisions that are more systematic and precise.
- Test results can predict future employee performance and reduce uncertainty.
- More accurate descriptions of people and their performance can be produced.

A number of difficulties are associated with personality assessment, including:

- **Predictive validity and reliability** – Can personality tests really predict with accuracy how people will behave in real life and can they take into account the complexity of people and situations? Can the personality test consistently achieve what it is claiming to measure?
- **The Barnum effect** – This is the name given to a type of subjective evaluation in which a person finds their own meaning but which could

apply to lots of people. When people are presented with a personality sketch or description of themselves, they can find meaning in the statements that could relate to anyone. The Barnum effect explains how people can be fooled by generic descriptions and highlights the limitations of personality assessment.

An example of a Barnum statement is as follows: 'You have a need for other people to like and admire you and yet you have a tendency to be critical of yourself. You have some personality weaknesses but are able to compensate for them. You have a wealth of unused capacity that you have not turned to your advantage. There are times that you have considerable doubts whether you have made the right decision or done the right thing.'

The 'Barnum effect' is an expression that appears to have originated from psychologist Paul Meehl (1956) in reference to P.T. Barnum. The circus owner Barnum had a reputation as a master psychological manipulator and is said to have claimed 'we have something for everybody'.

- **The 'self-report' problem** – The 'give them what they want' syndrome occurs when people are presented with a personality test. They already have a perception of the job they have applied for and the type of person that may be suitable. On the basis of this subjective evaluation, they complete the personality test and provide the answers that they think the organisation wants. For example, if a person is going for a job in sales, they may present themselves as being very sociable and outgoing because they believe this is what is wanted from them. The problem is that they may not be revealing their own traits.

- **'I'd like to be, so I'll say I am' syndrome** – People have aspirations about the type of person that they would like to be and the type of characteristics that they would like to possess. When being tested, people may describe who they would like to be rather than reveal the reality of their personality.

- **The self-awareness principle** – It is common that people have a low level of understanding about themselves. This serves as an ego-defensive mechanism, as they can maintain a stable view of their personality that is not threatened by constant evaluation and alteration. For many, the unexamined personality is much easier to deal with.

- **The 'construct validity' problem** – This addresses the issue of whether the personality test measures the variables or constructs that it is designed to measure. The test results may be affected by a person's mood, aspirations and assumptions, which question their validity. In other words, does the test measure what it's meant to, that is personality traits?

Other concerns about personality assessment include:

- Whether there is a direct causal link between personality type and performance in the workplace.
- If the use of personality tests could be an infringement of an individual's privacy.
- If testing could lead to social engineering and organisational control.

In addition, practice may have an effect on results; tests may be time-consuming and expensive and must be undertaken by those who are professionally qualified, to avoid misuse. However, personality tests provide benefits in that they offer the individual a greater understanding of themselves and identify areas for development. The use of testing can also reveal the strengths and weaknesses within a group of people and lead to the production of a balanced team in the workplace.

5.6 Conclusion

Personality is complex, but it is understood to consist of relatively stable and enduring traits that shape a person's behaviour. Personality has a significant impact on how employees interact with each other, whether they like working in teams or alone, their rate and quality of work. The Big Five model provides an insight for managers into the relationship between personality and job performance, but situational factors still need to be taken into consideration. Personality traits can be used to promote job performance and leadership effectiveness, and to enhance job satisfaction and motivation. Managers need to appreciate the challenges of personality assessment and to use the results wisely to inform and guide their decisions.

Summary

- Definition and nature of personality.
- The Big Five personality factors and personality-related characteristics.
- Personality testing.

Theory to real life

1. Identify the main characteristics that reflect your personality.
2. How do these characteristics influence the way you think, feel and behave?

3. Do you believe these characteristics are the result of your genetic inheritance or have they been influenced by your life experiences?
4. Describe, using the Big Five model, how a manager's personality may affect their behaviour towards employees.
5. How can personality assist a manager in understanding the reasons people behave the way they do in the workplace?
6. What advice would you provide to a manager about the use of personality tests as a method of selection?

Exercises

1. Assess your own personality
   Complete this short personality assessment, which is an example of the type of questionnaire developed by Eysenck.

For each question, choose yes or no.	**Yes**	**No**
1　Do you sometimes feel happy, sometimes depressed, without any apparent reason?	☐	☐
2　Do you have frequent ups and downs in mood either with or without apparent cause?	☐	☐
3　Are you inclined to be moody?	☐	☐
4　Does your mind often wander while you are trying to concentrate?	☐	☐
5　Are you frequently 'lost in thought' even when supposed to be taking part in a conversation?	☐	☐
6　Are you sometimes bubbling over with energy and sometimes very sluggish?	☐	☐
7　Do you prefer action to planning for action?	☐	☐
8　Are you happiest when you get involved in some project that calls for rapid action?	☐	☐

---

9 Do you usually take the initiative in making new friends? □ □

10 Are you inclined to be quick and sure in your actions? □ □

11 Would you rate yourself as a lively individual? □ □

12 Would you be very unhappy if you were prevented from making numerous social contacts? □ □

Source: Eysenck and Wilson (1975)

Scoring: A 'Yes' answer in any of the first six questions scores one point towards emotionality, while a 'No' answer does not score at all. Similarly, a 'Yes' answer to any of the last six items scores one point towards extroversion. You can therefore end up with two scores, either of which may run from 0 (very stable, very introverted) to 6 (very unstable emotionally, very extroverted). The majority of people will have scores of 2, 3 or 4, indicating moderate degrees of emotionality or extroversion.

What did you learn about personality from completing the extraversion–introversion questionnaire?

Essay questions

1. Briefly describe the nature of human personality.
2. The Big Five theory of personality helps us to understand the main differences in personality between people. Examine each of the following Big Five factors: emotional stability, extroversion, openness to experience, agreeableness and conscientiousness.
3. Explain the reasons why personality tests may not be accurate indicators of an individual's behaviour in the workplace.
4. Describe how knowledge about personality could be useful to managers in organisations.

Short questions

1. Propose a definition of personality.
2. The _____ versus _____ debate is about whether an individual's personality is shaped primarily by their genes or by their environment.
3. Which of the following is not included in the Big Five model?
   a. Agreeableness
   b. Conscientiousness
   c. Expressiveness
   d. Openness
4. Michael, one of the newest employees in the organisation, is an extrovert. Which of the following statements is least likely to be true?
   a. Michael will probably have a large network of friends.
   b. Michael will perform well on specialised, detail-oriented tasks.
   c. Michael will be suited to a managerial or sales position.
5. Introverts direct their energies _____ to their own thoughts, feelings and ideas.
6. Which dimension of personality is characterised by a tendency to be pleasant and accommodating in social situations?
7. Name each of the Big Five personality factors (hint: OCEAN).
8. Explain briefly the difference between an individual who has an internal locus of control and an individual who has an external locus of control.
9. Identify one problem associated with the use of personality tests.
10. Name one way in which an understanding of personality can benefit a manager in a workplace.

6
STRESS IN THE WORKPLACE

Objectives

This chapter will help you to:

- Define stress.
- Describe the General Adaptation Syndrome.
- Identify the difference between eustress and distress.
- Characterise Type A and B personality profiles.
- Examine the causes of life and organisational stressors.
- Understand the consequences of stress to the individual and the organisation.
- Recommend individual and organisational coping strategies.

6.1 Stress defined

Stress is complex and the experience of it is very individual due to its many causes and consequences. Stress is a reality of life in general and therefore part of the experience of work. The most important aspect of stress is managing it effectively.

The benefits for organisations in creating a work environment that helps employees manage the demands of life within and without the workplace include healthier employees, reduced absenteeism, increased productivity and an enhanced reputation.

According to Moorhead and Griffin (2012), stress can be defined as '**a person's adaptive response to a stimulus that places excessive psychological or physical demands on that person**'. The source of stress must be perceived by the person to be excessive.

Wagner and Hollenbeck (2010) assert that stress is '**an unpleasant emotional state**'.

Arroba and James (1991) state that stress is '**a person's response to an inappropriate level of pressure. It is a response to pressure, not the pressure itself.**' This description of stress highlights the fact that stress is caused by pressure from many different sources, such as peer pressure, financial pressure or exam pressure. It is when an individual believes that the pressure they are under is too much for them to handle that stress is experienced. When placed under a lot of pressure, some people experience no stress and others only need a small amount of pressure to suffer the side effects of stress. How the individual perceives the pressure and their ability to cope with the situation determine the level of stress they experience. Factors that create differences between people in relation to their experience of stress include perception, personality, social support, lifestyles and past experiences.

6.2 General Adaptation Syndrome

In 1936, the Hungarian endocrinologist Hans Selye (1907–82) described the body's reaction to stressful situations. As early as his second year of medical school (1926), he began developing his theory about how stress affects people's ability to cope with and adapt to the pressures of injury and disease. Selye (1946) discovered that patients with a range of ailments manifested many similar symptoms, which he ultimately attributed to the body's efforts to respond to the stresses of being ill. He called this collection of symptoms, this separate stress disease, stress syndrome or the **General Adaptation Syndrome (GAS).**

Selye stated that a stressful experience can be strong enough and last long enough to cause physical consequences that are harmful to good health and can lead to infection, illness, disease and death. He noted that each person resists the effects of stress in their own particular way but reaches a threshold or a point when their ability to cope is not as effective and stress begins to have an effect on them mentally and physically.

The General Adaptation Syndrome is made up of three distinct stages:

1. **Alarm reaction** – The person becomes aware of the stressor and the body mobilises the available resources to help cope with the experience. A general alarm is sent to all bodily systems. A stressor can be anything that can cause the stress response; for example, a person, object or situation. The body gets ready for 'fight or flight', preparing it for life-threatening situations, channelling resources away from areas such as the digestive and immune systems to more immediate muscular and emotional needs. This leads to the immune system being depressed, making people susceptible to disease. During the alarm reaction stage, the individual becomes more alert and the heart rate and blood pressure rise, with an increased level of respiration and blood flow to the muscles.

2. **Resistance** – In the second stage, a resistance to the stress is built. Bodily resources are at maximum use. The body attempts to return to normal and regain a state of balance. As we become used to the stress levels, we initially become *more* resistant to disease, which leads us to believe we can easily adapt to these more stressful situations. However, this is only

the immune system fighting to keep up with demands and expectations and it is working at abnormally high levels. Selye referred to this stage of GAS as 'the full war effort'. The individual must find some way of dealing with the stress.

3. **Exhaustion** – If the stress lasts sufficiently long, the body eventually enters a stage of exhaustion, a type of ageing due to 'wear and tear'. With very prolonged stress, bodily systems are ineffective. The immune system collapses and the likelihood of experiencing stress-related diseases increases. The body gives up trying to cope with a high level of stress. Parts of the body literally start to break down and people may become very unwell at this stage and the effects on health can be serious.

6.3 Eustress and distress

Stress can be the cause of stimulation and motivation and can have a positive effect on people's lives, but it can also cause upset and frustration.

Selye (1956) came up with the idea of eustress, which is an ideal amount of stress necessary to keep the body's immune system in tune, but not enough to overwhelm it. He called positive stress *eustress* and negative stress *distress*.

Eustress enhances function (physical or mental, such as through strength training or challenging work), whereas persistent stress that is not resolved through coping or adaptation is termed distress and may lead to escape (anxiety) or withdrawal (depression) behaviour.

Eustress can be defined as a *pleasant stress* that accompanies positive events. It can produce energy, enthusiasm and motivation. People cannot avoid stress and sometimes may not want to. Controlled stress can give individuals a competitive edge in their performance.

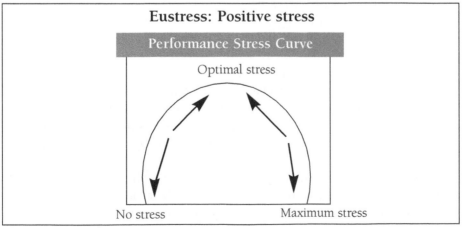

Figure 6.1 A performance stress curve in eustress

The stress curve diagram in Figure 6.1 demonstrates that for any performance-related activity, an optimal level of stress exists. When taking part in an interview, the candidate benefits from a certain amount of stress, as it provides focus that helps them to think clearly and quickly and to express thoughts in a way that will give them a competitive edge.

Distress can be defined as *unpleasant stress* that accompanies negative events, such as conflict at home or in the workplace. This is harmful stress. It causes frustration and upset and may have negative consequences for an individual's well-being.

6.4 Type A and B personality profiles

Individuals differ in their resilience to stress and their susceptibility to stress-related illnesses. This fact was investigated in 1959 by cardiologists Meyer Friedman and R.H. Rosenman. Type A behaviour was first described as a potential risk factor in coronary disease. After a nine-year study of over 3,000 healthy men aged 35 to 59, Friedman and Rosenman estimated that Type A behaviour doubles the risk of coronary heart disease in otherwise healthy individuals.

The **Type A personality** is a set of characteristics that includes being impatient, excessively time-conscious, insecure about one's status, highly competitive, hostile and aggressive, and incapable of relaxation. Type A individuals are often high-achieving workaholics who multi-task, drive themselves with deadlines and are unhappy about the smallest of delays.

Typically, a Type A personality is impatient, hurries, is under pressure, prompt and often early for appointments, watches the clock, walks/talks/eats rapidly, does multiple activities simultaneously, lives in the future, is always planning and feels that 'there's never enough time'. According to Lee *et al.* (1990), employees with a Type A personality experience high levels of job satisfaction and performance aligned with high reported incidents of health complaints.

Jackson (1988) found that Type A managers, due to the fast pace that they work at, do not make thoughtful analyses of complex issues. Also, they cause those around them to experience stress and discomfort due to their impatience and hostility. Therefore, the most successful top executives have a Type B personality, which is characterised by patience and good interpersonal skills.

The **Type B personality** is relaxed, easy-going, unpressured and confident. They readily focus on the quality of their life, are easy-going, take 'one day at a time' and are less ambitious and less irritable than the Type A person.

There is also a Type AB mixed profile for people who cannot be clearly categorised and have a combination of both types of personality.

The research undertaken by Friedman and Rosenman had a big influence in stimulating the development of the field of health psychology, in which psychologists look at how a person's mental state affects their physical health.

6.5 Causes of stress

Factors in and out of the workplace can produce stress. It is important to understand both organisational and life stressors, as they can have a significant effect on the performance of employees.

Organisational stressors

Four general sets of organisational stressors have been identified by Moorhead and Griffin (2012) as task demands, physical demands, role demands and interpersonal demands.

Task demands

The nature of a job, the environment, expected behaviours and other people all place demands on individuals in the workplace.

- **Specific job** – By their very nature, some occupations are more stressful than others. This relates to the amount of pressure placed on an employee. Jobs that are demanding include being an air traffic controller, a customer service agent or a stockbroker.
- **Physical threats** – When an individual experiences threats to their physical well-being, this places additional pressure on them. This is the case for coal miners, firefighters, those in the armed services and many others.
- **Job security** – People need to feel secure in the workplace. If uncertainty exists about their employment and subsequent pay, the individual may experience stress due to feelings of insecurity.
- **Overload** – This occurs when employees are expected to complete more tasks than their time and/or ability allow and they may feel under pressure and experience stress. *Quantitative overload* is caused by an individual having too much to do and too little time to complete the task-related activities. *Qualitative overload* may be experienced if employees do not have the appropriate knowledge, skills or abilities required to do the job.
- **Underload** – If a person has too little to do and too much time to do it,

they experience *quantitative underload*. Being overqualified for a job may mean that an employee may encounter *qualitative underload*. The consequences of underload include boredom, apathy, a lack of participation, increased absenteeism and being prone to injury.

Physical demands

The setting or environment of the workplace may contribute to stress levels. Factors that put pressure on individuals include extremes of temperature, poor lighting and poor office design. Open-plan layouts in offices can produce stress because they can be noisy, are not conducive to undertaking quiet work that requires concentration and do not provide much privacy for meetings or phone calls. However, when employees are provided with individual office space this can lead to feelings of isolation, difficulties meeting social needs and problems in sharing knowledge and lack of joint problem-solving.

Role demands

Demands are placed on employees due to role ambiguity and role conflict.

- **Role ambiguity** – This is experienced when an individual is uncertain as to what is expected of them in a particular role, the expectations of other people and the exact nature of the job. The result is stress, insecurity and loss of self-confidence and self-esteem. It is important that employees are clear about the scope and responsibilities of their job.
- **Role conflict** – This occurs when expectations about a role contradict each other. Inter-role and intra-role conflict are sources of stress.
  - **Inter-role conflict** – This is a common cause of stress and occurs when conflict exists between two or more roles that people play in their lives. Students experience inter-role conflict as they juggle their studies, work, family responsibilities, sporting interests, hobbies and social life.
  - **Intra-role conflict** – Within the same role there may be contradictions that cause anxiety. For example, a manager is faced with the need to provide people with clear instructions about the activities that need to be undertaken and to monitor results closely. At the same time, the manager is keen to develop a friendly and trusting relationship with employees. Among the many roles that people have, they attempt to undertake roles which at times may conflict with one another. For example, the roles of parent and friend may cause conflict.

Kahn *et al.* (1964) report that role conflict is associated with high levels of interpersonal tension and poor interpersonal relations; reduced job satisfaction; decreased confidence in the organisation; and lower levels of commitment to the organisation.

Interpersonal demands

Working with other people is a cause of stress. There may be group pressures to maintain particular attitudes and to perform to a certain level. The leadership style may be one that is too directive and task-oriented or may be more relationship-oriented. The management style may or may not suit the employees. Finally, stress can be caused by the personality characteristics of others and how these are manifested in their behaviour. Some people may be very loud, talking and laughing a lot of the time, which may annoy others. On the other hand, some employees may be very quiet and avoid contact, which frustrates other people. Clashes and conflicts between personality types can cause conflict. Individual habits and behaviours also produce stress, including smoking, swearing, chewing gum and bad manners, all of which demonstrate a lack of consideration for others.

Life stressors

Two central categories of life stress have been identified as **life change** and **life trauma.**

In 1967, psychiatrists Thomas Holmes and Richard Rahe examined the medical records of over 5,000 medical patients in order to determine whether stressful life events might lead to illnesses. They believed that changes associated with major life events absorb energy and reduce the ability of the body to defend itself from illness.

Life change

Holmes and Rahe (1967) developed the *Social Readjustment Rating Scale* in which they attempted to identify life changes that people encounter and to understand the effect on health. Life change is described as any meaningful change in a person's personal or work life. Change is thought to lead to stress and eventually disease.

To measure stress according to the Social Readjustment Rating Scale, the number of life change units, which apply to events that have taken place in the past year of an individual's life, are added up. The final score gives an estimate of how stress affects health and indicates the likelihood of illness in the following year.

Life event	Life change units
Death of a spouse	100
Divorce	73
Marital breakdown or separation	65
Imprisonment	63
Death of a close family member	63
Personal injury or illness	53
Getting married	50
Dismissal from work	47
Marital reconciliation	45
Retirement	45
Change in health of family member	44
Pregnancy	40
Sexual difficulties	39
Gain a new family member	39
Business readjustment	39
Change in financial state	38
Change in frequency of arguments	35
Taking on a major mortgage	32
Foreclosure of mortgage or loan	30
Change in responsibilities at work	29
Child leaving home	29
Trouble with in-laws	29
Outstanding personal achievement	28
Spouse starts or stops work	26
Begin or finish school	26
Change in living conditions	25
Revision of personal habits	24
Trouble with boss	23
Change in working hours or conditions	20
Change in residence	20
Change in schools	20
Change in recreation	19
Change in church activities	19
Change in social activities	18
Taking on a minor mortgage or loan	17
Change in sleeping habits	16
Change in number of family reunions	15
Change in eating habits	15
Vacation	13
Christmas	12
Minor violation of the law	11

> Score of 300 and over: At risk of illness.
> Score of 150–299 and over: Risk of illness is moderate (reduced by 30 per cent from the above risk).
> Score 150 or less: Only a slight risk of illness.
>
> Source: Holmes and Rahe (1967)

Table 6.1 Social Readjustment Rating Scale

Life trauma

The causes of life trauma have a narrower, more direct and short-term focus. They represent single incidents or upheavals that affect attitudes, emotions and behaviour. Life traumas that may cause stress include family difficulties and health problems that are initially unrelated to stress. The effects of these experiences will impact on the performance of the employee.

6.6 Consequences of stress

The results of stress are experienced by both the individual and the organisation and collectively in the form of burnout.

Individual consequences

- **Behavioural** – When experiencing stress, individuals adapt their behaviour. This change may be negative and could result in harm being caused to themselves or others. Behavioural changes include fidgeting, rudeness towards others, increased smoking and consumption of alcohol and/or other drugs, violence, changes in eating patterns, absenteeism and a greater frequency of accidents.
- **Psychological** – Stress has an effect on our mental health and detracts from feelings of well-being. This can lead to depression, insomnia, loss of confidence and reduced self-esteem. According to Fletcher (1988), if people are unable to alter or get away from the source of stress, they may use psychological substitutes such as anger, criticism, denial, apathy, fantasy, hopelessness and forgetfulness.
- **Medical** – The person's physical well-being may be adversely affected and stress-related conditions and health problems may be experienced. These include allergies, headaches, backaches, ulcers, gastrointestinal disorders, skin conditions such as acne, hives and eczema, high blood pressure, heart disease and stroke.

Organisational consequences

- **Performance** – Stress can cause a decline in the quality and quantity of work undertaken by individuals and groups in organisations. When people feel under pressure, they may make poor decisions and are more likely to become involved in conflict.
- **Withdrawal** – Employees' withdrawal from the workplace may be demonstrated by high levels of absenteeism and turnover as people feel that they cannot cope with the level of stress. Withdrawal is not always physical; it can also be psychological. Individuals are present in the workplace but are not as engaged or as enthusiastic as they may have been previously.
- **Attitudes** – Stress may produce a negative attitude and have an impact on the level of job satisfaction experienced, morale, commitment and motivation. Employees may complain about issues that were not previously a cause of concern and this may result in them performing at a low level in order to just get by.

Burnout

This serious consequence of stress affects both the individual and the organisation. The term 'burnout' was coined by Herbert Freudenberger in 1974 in his book *Burnout: The High Cost of High Achievement*. Burnout was originally defined by Freudenberger as '*the extinction of motivation or incentive, especially where one's devotion to a cause or relationship fails to produce the desired results*'.

There are several factors that can contribute to burnout, including job-related aspects, lifestyle factors and personality characteristics. Burnout produces a general feeling of exhaustion. It occurs when an individual simultaneously experiences increased pressure and decreased sources of satisfaction. Those who are likely to experience burnout tend to have high aspirations and strong motivation.

Burnout is caused by prolonged stress, fatigue, frustration and feelings of helplessness. People experience overwhelming demands and, as they become more stressed, over time their aspirations and motivation decrease. This results in a loss of self-confidence and signs of withdrawal. The individual may dread going to work, take longer to accomplish tasks and display signs of mental and physical exhaustion.

Classic symptoms of burnout include:

- **Depleted physical energy** – Prolonged stress can be physically draining and may cause individuals to feel tired much of the time and to feel that they no longer have the energy they once did.
- **Emotional exhaustion** – People may become impatient, moody, inexplicably sad or just get frustrated more easily than they normally would.
- **Lowered immunity to illness** – When people experience high levels of stress for a prolonged amount of time, the immune system suffers. People who are suffering from burnout usually get the message from their body that something needs to change and that message comes in the form of increased susceptibility to colds and other minor illnesses and at times some more serious ones.
- **Less investment in interpersonal relationships** – Withdrawing to varying extents from interpersonal relationships is another likely sign of burnout. Individuals may feel like they have less to give, that they are less interested in having fun or just less patient with people.
- **Increasingly pessimistic outlook** – When experiencing burnout, it is more difficult to get excited about life, to expect the best, to let things roll off your back and in general to 'look on the bright side'. Optimism is a great buffer against stress and those suffering from burnout find it harder to get out of the rut than they normally would.
- **Increased absenteeism and inefficiency at work** – When experiencing job burnout, it gets more difficult for individuals just to get out of bed and face more of what has been overwhelming them in the first place. This may be an unconscious defence mechanism against burnout, but those experiencing it tend to be less effective overall and stay home from work more frequently. This could also be due to increased illness due to lowered immunity. This is part of why it makes sense for workers to take some time off *before* they feel burnt out and why it makes sense for employers not to run their workers into the ground.

Burnout can be prevented by removing personal, job and organisational stressors. Buffers can be used by organisations to reduce the symptoms of burnout, which involve additional resources and/or administrative changes. Buffers include extra employees or resources at busy periods; support from management; recognition for achievements; participation in decision-making; equity in reward systems; and changes in roles and responsibilities.

6.7 Coping strategies

It is vital that both the individual and the organisation develop and implement coping strategies to deal with stress. Lazarus and Folkman (1984) describe coping as '*the process of managing demands (external or internal) that are appraised as taxing or exceeding the resources of the person*'. Coping strategies help to reduce or eliminate the negative consequences of stress which can have such a negative impact on the individual's quality of life and organisational performance. Coping strategies act as a buffer between the causes of stress and the consequences. Strategies have been developed to assist both individuals and organisations to manage stress (Kelly, 1997).

Individual coping strategies

It is important that individuals take responsibility and learn to cope with stress effectively. Coping strategies include:

- **Adequate exercise, rest and nutrition** – Adequate exercise, rest and nutrition are central to developing resistance to stress. Exercise including walking, swimming, hiking and other active sports is encouraged. Activities such as these relieve tension and anxiety and produce feelings of confidence and optimism. People do not always realise the importance of sleep; if they do not get adequate sleep, they are less able to handle stress and are less productive. Individuals who get inadequate sleep on a regular basis put themselves into a state of chronic sleep deprivation and *chronic stress*, and put themselves at a higher risk of burnout. Nutrition involves a balanced diet.
- **Relaxation** – When individuals are involved in work, study or any other type of activity, break times should be structured into their work plan. A break from an activity can provide refreshing results and can be for a few minutes or for a few hours. Break times could include body stretching, a brief glance at your surroundings, a snack or changing to another activity. Relaxation helps people to adapt to stress and to return to a task relaxed and refreshed.
- **Time management** – To reduce stress, it is important to manage time effectively. A method that can be used is to list the work that needs to be undertaken into critical, important or optional/trivial activities. In this way, focus can be given to the important tasks and less important tasks can be done at a later time or delegated to others. By ticking off the completed tasks on the list a sense of achievement and confidence is created, which encourages further action.

- **Role management** – People need to reduce the effects of stress by more effectively managing their role in the workplace. This involves avoiding task overload or underload, role ambiguity and conflict. For many it may simply involve learning to say 'no'.
- **Support groups** – Individuals need people to help them shoulder the emotional burdens in their lives in and out of the workplace. Being able to talk to someone in the family, a friend or colleague about the causes of stress, someone to enjoy free time with, and someone to be understanding when times are tough and to supply new ideas when inspiration is lacking are all important and necessary aspects of social support. When people feel isolated with their stress, this creates *more stress* and increases the risk of burnout, whereas adequate social support can be a buffer against it.
- **Increased self-awareness** – Individuals should gain an understanding of how they normally behave in the workplace and other social situations. This self-awareness will help them to identify the signs that indicate they are becoming stressed. Such knowledge will provide the person with the opportunity to make choices about how to manage the situation effectively and reduce the amount of stress experienced.

Organisational coping strategies

Organisations need to provide interventions to help employees to cope with stress because the organisation itself may contribute to the stress experienced by employees and therefore has a duty of care. Moreover, employees are more productive when experiencing lower levels of stress. Coping strategies include:

- **Well-designed jobs** – Organisations should ensure that employees have the relevant qualifications and experience to complete the required task-related activities; that not too much or too little work is given to any one person; and that clarity exists about roles and responsibilities in the workplace in order to reduce stress.
- **Work schedules** – It is central to people's mental and physical well-being that they achieve a good *work–life balance*. Of course, everyone will have a very busy week at times, but those who devote all their time to work and work-related activities and put other areas of their lives, such as relationships, hobbies and exercise, on hold place themselves at a higher risk of burnout. Initiatives such as flexitime, jobsharing, teleworking and shorter working weeks and others that give employees more choice over working patterns should be considered to reduce stress. *The Quality of Working Life Survey,* published by the Chartered Management Institute in

2001, revealed that 91 per cent of managers regularly exceeded their contracted hours. Three-quarters of the managers asked said working late or at weekends was the only way to deal with their workload, while two-thirds believed it was a part of their organisation's culture.

- **Organisational culture** – Deal and Kennedy (1982) define culture as 'the way we do things around here'. The normal, or usual, way some organisations function can cause stress. Norms may exist about the ease or difficulty of taking time off; working long hours; heavy workloads; acceptable levels of conflict; and the amount of consideration given to an employee's family situation and non-work activities. These ways of working, which cause stress, should be identified and appropriate changes made to reduce the occurrence of stress. The longer employees stay at the office, the less time they give to their personal life. The less time they give to their personal life, the more likely domestic problems are to occur, leading to stress at home on top of stress at work. An organisational culture that incorporates a participative style of management can reduce the level of stress experienced (Ivancevich *et al.*, 1990).

- **Supervision** – Depending on the style of leadership, employees can feel recognised for their achievements, supported when they have difficulties and valued. Alternatively, they can feel unappreciated, unrecognised, unfairly treated and insecure in their position. Supervisors need to help employees to cope with the difficulties experienced in the workplace and support achievements. They need to constantly adapt their style to suit the employee and the situation. Fox *et al.* (1993) identified a number of behaviours that can provoke stress:
  - Giving inconsistent instructions.
  - Failing to provide physical and emotional support.
  - Lacking concern for the well-being of employees.
  - Failing to provide adequate direction.
  - Placing too strong an emphasis on productivity.
  - Focusing on isolated examples of substandard performance.
  - Failing to recognise good performance.

- **Stress management and health promotion programmes** – Organisations can develop programmes to specifically target stress. This may include providing employees with the opportunity to be involved in a stress-management course. Also, it may take the form of wellness programmes to encourage employees to stop smoking, to reduce alcohol consumption, to exercise more and to take responsibility for their physical and mental health. Additional interventions used by some companies include a duvet day (where an employee is given one to two days a year when they can take time out), access to health and fitness centres and career breaks.

Employers should take stress seriously. They need to investigate stress levels and the causes, ensure employees are well matched to their jobs, establish clear objectives, provide training, consider the introduction of flexible working hours, provide opportunities for staff development and be supportive on a daily basis.

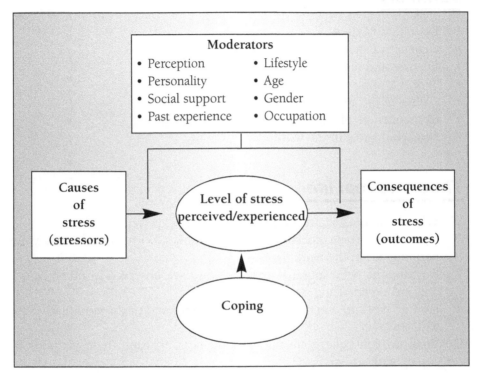

Figure 6.2 Model of stress

6.8 Conclusion

Stress is an individual's adaptive response to a level of pressure that is perceived to be excessive. Factors that moderate the level of stress experienced include perception, personality, social support, past experience, lifestyle, age, gender and occupation. The three stages of response to stress identified within the General Adaptation Syndrome are alarm reaction, resistance and exhaustion. Both positive stress, eustress, and negative stress, distress, exist and have a motivational effect on people. An individual's experience of stress is understood to be affected by whether they have a Type A or B personality. Stress is caused by many factors related to the workplace, but also by a wide range of life experiences. The consequences of stress are seen at both individual and organisational levels. It is of critical importance that both employees and the organisation develop and implement coping strategies to deal with stress and promote well-being.

Summary

- Definition of stress.
- General Adaptation Syndrome.
- Eustress and distress.
- Type A and B personality profiles.
- Causes of life and organisational stressors.
- Consequences of stress.
- Managing stress in the workplace.

Theory to real life

1. What symptoms of stress do you commonly experience?
2. How does stress affect your relationships with others and your performance in the workplace?
3. Describe the behavioural symptoms you have observed in others when they are experiencing stress.
4. How do you and others around you in college and/or the workplace cope with stress?
5. What do you believe are the consequences of using these methods of coping with stress?
6. In your opinion, what should schools/colleges/organisations/government do to help people understand more about stress?
7. Have you used any stress-reduction techniques? Did you find them effective?

Exercises

1. Complete the Type A–B personality type questionnaire.

Where are you on the Type A–B Behaviour Continuum?

Instructions

For each question, indicate the extent to which each statement is true of you.

	Not at all true of me	Neither very true nor very untrue of me	Very true of me

1. I hate giving up before I'm absolutely sure that I'm licked.

   1 — 2 — 3 — 4 — 5

2. Sometimes I feel that I shouldn't be working so hard, but something drives me on.

   1 — 2 — 3 — 4 — 5

3. I thrive on challenging situations. The more challenges I have, the better.

   1 — 2 — 3 — 4 — 5

4. In comparison to most people I know, I'm very involved in my work.

   1 — 2 — 3 — 4 — 5

5. It seems as if I need 30 hours a day to finish all the things I'm faced with.

   1 — 2 — 3 — 4 — 5

6. In general, I approach my work more seriously than most people I know.

   1 — 2 — 3 — 4 — 5

7. I guess there are some people who can be nonchalant about their work, but I'm not one of them.

   1 — 2 — 3 — 4 — 5

8. My achievements are considered to be significantly higher than those of most people I know.

   1 — 2 — 3 — 4 — 5

9. I've often been asked to be an officer of some group or groups.

   1 — 2 — 3 — 4 — 5

Total score = _____

Arbitrary Norms
Type B = 9–22
Balanced Type A and B = 23–35
Type A = 36–45

Source: Caplan *et al.* (1975)

2. Are you a Type A or Type B person? What impact does your style of personality have on the way in which you work?
3. In class, discuss the main sources of stress affecting people, the consequences experienced and common methods of coping that are used.

Essay questions

1. Provide a definition of stress.
2. Investigate the main causes of life and organisational stressors.
3. Explain the consequences of stress for the individual and the organisation.
4. Examine the coping methods that can be used by individuals and organisations to deal with stress in a positive manner.

Short questions

1. Stress is an individual's response to an inappropriate level of pressure. TRUE/FALSE?
2. What are the three stages in Seyle's General Adaptation Syndrome?
3. What is eustress?
4. What is distress?
5. How does a Type A person deal with stress?
6. How does a Type B person deal with stress?
7. Name two organisational sources of stress.
8. Identify two medical consequences of stress.
9. Name an organisational consequence of stress.
10. Name two individual methods of coping with stress.
11. Identify a method that organisations use to help employees cope with stress.

7
MOTIVATION

Objectives

This chapter will help you to:

- Propose a definition of motivation.
- Appreciate the importance of the study of motivation in creating an effective organisation.
- Identify the differences between the content and process approaches to motivation.
- Describe Maslow's Hierarchy of Needs.
- Recognise the contribution made by Herzberg to understanding motivation in the workplace.
- Examine the importance of the equitable treatment of people in the workplace.
- Understand the significance of positively influencing employees' expectations.

7.1 Motivation defined

Motivation is a force that causes people to engage in behaviour that results in the satisfaction of individual needs. An employee's level of motivation influences the effort they put into their work and therefore increases the standard of the output.

According to Moorhead and Griffin (2012), '**motivation is the set of forces that leads people to behave in particular ways**'.

Bratton *et al.* (2010) state that motivation can be defined as '**the forces within a person that affect his or her direction, intensity and persistence of voluntary behaviour**'.

Williams (1981) highlighted the complex nature of motivation and the stages involved in the process. He described motivation as the interrelationship between needs, behaviour aimed at overcoming needs and the fulfilment of needs.

When factors that determine the motivation of employees in the workplace are proposed, most people immediately think of a high salary. This answer is correct, as some employees will be motivated by money, but fails to consider other factors motivating people in the workplace, such as security, belongingness and achievement. Human motivation is a personal characteristic, and there is no one best way to understand it or one method of management to implement that will suit all the people all the time.

Why do we need motivated employees? The answer is survival (Smith, 1994). Motivated employees are needed in our rapidly changing workplaces to help organisations survive. In addition, motivated employees are more productive.

Motivation influences the output of every business and concerns both quantity and quality. Employees are an organisation's greatest asset and no matter how efficient its technology and equipment may be, this is no match for the effectiveness and efficiency of its staff.

The role of the manager in the workplace is to achieve goals through other people. In order to achieve results, a manager should have the ability to motivate employees. In spite of extensive research into motivation, it is not clearly understood and is often not practised. To gain an insight into motivation, an understanding of human nature is required. Understanding people and individual differences, however, is a complex study, but an appreciation of these is fundamental to effective employee motivation and therefore the processes of management and leadership.

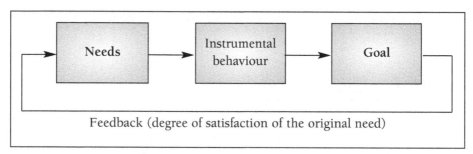

Figure 7.1 The process of motivation

Performance is considered to be a function of motivation, ability and environment (Vroom, 1964). Performance depends on:

$$P = f(M, A + E)$$

Where:
    P = Performance
    M = Motivation
    A = Ability
    E = Environment

7.2 Theories of motivation

Although there is no one best way to understand motivation, collectively the different theories provide a framework within which to examine the challenge of how to most effectively motivate people at work. The relevance of each of these theories will be particular to each work situation.

Motivational theories attempt to answer the question of what motivates people and in particular to examine the reasons why people select a particular course of action or behaviour in preference to others. The history of research into motivation has witnessed the emergence of differing but not mutually exclusive approaches to motivation. Many competing theories exist that attempt to explain the nature of motivation. These theories are all at least partially valid and help explain the behaviour of some people some of the time. However, the search for a generalised theory of motivation at work is an endless quest. Even though the theories presented in this chapter have their critics, any theory or study that provides an understanding of how best to motivate people at work is useful.

Content vs. process approaches to motivation

The **content theories** are also referred to as the *need theories*. They attempt to explain the factors within a person that energise, direct and stop behaviour. The fundamental assumption underlying content theories is that need deficiencies cause behaviour. In general, they focus on the specific factors that motivate people and some examine the determinants of employee motivation. The content theories attempt to answer the question, 'What motivates people?'

The **process theories** attempt to examine how personal or individual factors (internal to the person) interact and influence each other to produce certain types of behaviour. The main focus of this approach is on how behaviour is initiated, directed and sustained. The process theories present answers to the question, 'How does each invdivdual satisfy their needs?'

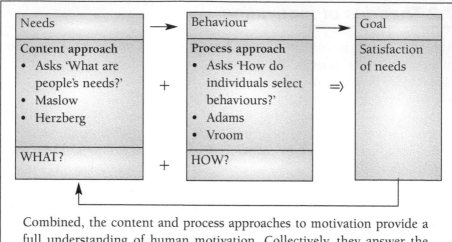

Figure 7.2 The content and process approaches to motivation

7.3 Content theories

Maslow's Hierarchy of Needs theory and Herzberg's Two-factor theory are content theories of motivation and therefore examine what people's needs are in the workplace.

Maslow's Hierarchy of Needs

Abraham Maslow developed the Hierarchy of Needs model in the USA in the 1940s and 1950s, and the Hierarchy of Needs theory remains valid today for understanding human motivation, management training and personal development.

Abraham Maslow published *A Theory of Human Motivation* in 1943; in it, he contended that people are wanting/needing beings. He proposed that individuals always want more and what they want depends on what they already have. Maslow categorised human needs and arranged them into a series of levels, or a hierarchy of importance. The most important needs are placed at the bottom of the hierarchy.

Fundamentally, people go through life seeking to satisfy these needs, starting with the physiological needs upwards. When a lower-order need is satisfied, the next need becomes dominant and individuals attempt to satisfy the next higher level of need. To motivate people, they must be provided with an opportunity to satisfy their current level of need. When that need is met or satisfied, it will no longer act as a significant motivator because only unmet or unsatisfied needs motivate people.

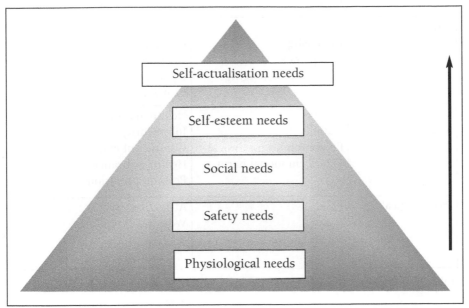

Figure 7.3 Maslow's Hierarchy of Needs

A common misunderstanding about the hierarchy is that each need must be fully satisfied before the next need arises. In actual fact, an individual will usually have degrees or percentages of satisfaction at each level. The greater this degree of satisfaction, the less influence on motivation a need will have.

Level of need	General rewards	Organisational factors
Self-actualisation	Growth Achievement of potential Advancement Self-fulfilment Becoming everything that one is capable of becoming What humans can be, they must be	Challenging job opportunities encouraging creativity Discretion over work activities Achievement in work Promotion ———▶

Self-esteem	Self-respect Autonomy Status Prestige	Social recognition Job title High status of job Regular feedback
Social	Love Friendship Acceptance Feelings of belonging	Work groups/teams Company sports/social clubs Friendly supervision Open communication Professional associations
Safety	Security Stability Protection from physical and emotional harm	Health and safety Job security Contract of employment Health insurance Pension provisions
Physiological	Food Water Sleep Sex	Attractive pay Working conditions

Table 7.1 Application of Maslow's Hierarchy of Needs in the workplace

Maslow's theory stimulated much research and thinking in the area of motivation. It created an awareness of the fact that behaviour is influenced by a number of different motives. The hierarchy also provided a very useful framework for the categorisation of needs. However, a number of problems with the theory exist. These include:

- The fact that rewards may satisfy more than one need.
- The questions of how progression can be measured.
- Whether the hierarchy has universal application.
- Whether the link between satisfaction of needs and enhanced performance can so easily be established.

Maslow's Hierarchy of Needs clearly identifies the responsibility of employers to provide a workplace environment that encourages and enables employees to fulfil their own unique potential (self-actualisation). The creation of such an environment will be of great benefit to the individual, the organisation and society.

Herzberg's Two-factor theory

Frederick Herzberg, an American psychologist, and his associates presented the **Two-factor theory** (also known as the *Hygiene-Motivation* theory) in 1959. He undertook his research into motivation by interviewing 203 American accountants and engineers, who were selected due to the growing importance of their professions in the business world. The *critical incident technique* was used and subjects were asked to relate times when they felt exceptionally good or bad about their present job or any previous job and to provide reasons and a description of the sequence of events that caused the positive or negative feeling.

The results of the research were consistent and demonstrated two different sets of factors influencing motivation at work. If absent or weak, the first set of factors causes dissatisfaction. They relate to the job environment or the context in which the job is done and are extrinsic to the job itself. Herzberg called these factors the *hygiene,* or maintenance, factors; they include pay and supervision.

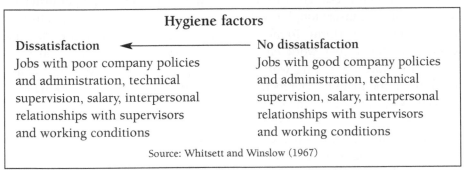

Figure 7.4 Hygiene factors

The second set of factors, which if present create feelings of job satisfaction, are based on an individual's need for personal growth. These factors can motivate an individual to increase effort and achieve above-average performance. They relate directly to the job itself and are intrinsic to the job. Herzberg named these the *motivators,* or *growth factors;* they include recognition and achievement.

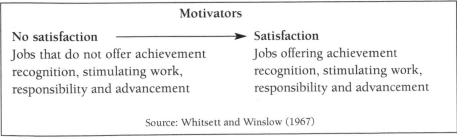

Figure 7.5 Motivators

Feelings of dissatisfaction and satisfaction exist at the same time and are equally important.

Hygiene factors	Motivators
Salary	Job security
Working conditions	Level and quality of supervision
Company policy and administration	Nature of work
Interpersonal relations	Recognition
Sense of achievement	Personal growth and advancement
Responsibility	

Table 7.2 Herzberg's Two-factor theory

Herzberg contends that good hygiene will only lead to average performance and prevent dissatisfaction, but will not on its own create a positive attitude or motivation to perform. To motivate employees, managers must enrich the content of the actual work employees are asked to undertake, such as providing more interesting work and giving more recognition. In making these recommendations, Herzberg coined the phrase 'quality of working life'.

Herzberg's Two-factor theory can be applied by managers by:

- Eliminating situations that cause job dissatisfaction.
- Implementing motivational factors.
- Vertically expanding jobs.

The consequences of demotivated employees include low productivity, poor production or service quality, complaints about pay and working conditions, breakdowns in employer–employee communications and relationships, industrial disputes and strikes.

Even though Herzberg's original studies have been repeated with different types of workers and results have proved consistent with the original research, the Two-factor theory has been criticised. The critics comment that a single factor may be a *satisfier* for one employee but cause *job dissatisfaction* for another; for example, increased responsibility may be welcomed by some and dreaded by others. In spite of the criticisms, Herzberg has made a valuable contribution to motivation research by drawing attention to the importance of *job design* in bringing about job enrichment. According to Herzberg, this can be achieved through job enlargement, job rotation and job enrichment and is highlighted in the phrase *'quality of working life'*.

Hierarchy of Needs vs. Two-factor theory

Comparisions can be drawn between Maslow's and Herzberg's theories.

Maslow	Herzberg
Self-actualisation	Motivators
Self-esteem	
Social	
Safety	Hygiene
Physiological	

Table 7.3 Comparision of Maslow's and Herzberg's theories

It can be contended that the lower-level needs of Maslow's hierarchy relate to the hygiene, or extrinsic, factors identified by Herzberg. In addition, comparisons can be drawn betweeen Maslow's higher-order needs and Herzberg's motivation factors. Connection can therefore be made between theories and the needs of people at work. The challenge of finding ways to increase levels of motivation at work remains. To achieve this, managers need to appreciate business theory, to understand their employees and to be creative in their approach to designing the work experience.

Other content theories

Additional content or need theories include:

- McClelland's (1961) need theory focuses on the need for achievement, affiliation and power.
- McGregor's (1960) Theory X Theory Y presents two contrasting sets of managerial assumptions about people. Theory X type managers assume that people dislike responsibility and lack ambition and therefore need to be led and controlled. Theory Y type managers believe that people seek responsibility, naturally want to work and are creative and ingenious in solving many organisational problems. These managerial styles affect the level of employee motivation.
- Alderfer's (1972) ERG theory describes three basic need categories: existence, relatedness and growth. This theory extends and refines Maslow's Hierarchy of Needs theory.

7.4 Process theories

Adams' **Equity theory** and **Vroom's Expectancy theory** are process theories of motivation and therefore examine how people and, in particular, employees satisfy their work-related needs.

Equity theory of motivation – Am I being treated fairly?

The workplace and behavioural psychologist J. Stacey Adams put forward his Equity theory in 1963. The Equity theory acknowledges that subtle and variable factors influence an individual's perception of their relationship with their work. *Equity* can be defined as the belief people have that they are being treated fairly in relation to others and provides people with a sense of what is fair and reasonable. *Inequity* is defined as the belief that people are being treated unfairly in relation to others. Equity evaluations are based on the exchange theory, as each employee seeks a fair balance between what they put into their job and what they get out of it. Adams believes that this involves the individual evaluating their inputs in relation to their outputs.

Inputs are a person's contributions to an organisation, such as effort, loyalty, knowledge, skill, ability, hard work, flexibility, commitment and enthusiasm. *Outputs* are what the individual receives in return for inputs, including pay, expenses, benefits, pension plans, bonuses, commission, recognition, praise, responsibility, training, sense of achievement and promotional opportunities.

Employees need to feel that there is a fair balance between their inputs and outputs. This is achieved as people engage in a *social comparison process* and compare their own inputs and outputs to other employees or referents in the marketplace. Employees are also affected by colleagues, friends and partners in identifying these benchmarks.

Referent	Categories
Others	Individuals with similar jobs, partners, friends, neighbours
System	Organisational pay policies, procedures and administration
Self	Input–output ratios unique to the individual (subjective evaluation)

Table 7.4 Referent categories used in making equity evaluations

When employees feel that their inputs are equitable and that they have been adequately rewarded by the outputs received, they experience job satisfaction and are motivated to continue performing at the same level. If, however, employees feel that their inputs are greater than their outputs and are therefore inequitable, they may become demotivated. It is important to note that an understanding of equity is based on subjectively perceived relativities and market norms and thus are prone to bias. In addition, this evaluation may not always be correct, since both tangible and intangible information is used in its formulation.

Individuals respond to this experience of inequity in different ways. Some will become inwardly unhappy and disgruntled and may reduce effort and application, whereas others may become visibly difficult and even exhibit disruptive behaviour. Some may look for another job or attempt to enhance their outputs by working harder, seeking more recognition or by making claims for better pay and conditions.

Managers should seek to find a fair balance between the inputs that an employee gives and the outputs received. According to Adams' Equity theory, the experience of equity serves to ensure a strong and productive relationship is achieved with employees and results in contented and motivated employees.

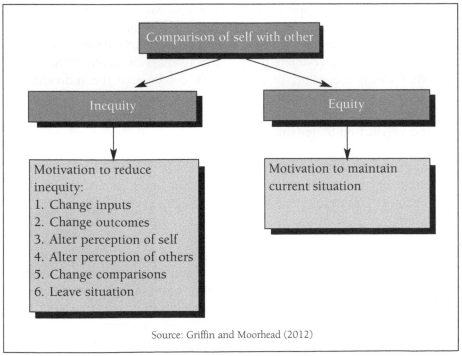

Source: Griffin and Moorhead (2012)

Figure 7.6 Adam's Equity theory – responses to perceptions of equity and inequity

Expectancy theory of motivation – What's in it for me?

Victor Vroom presented the Expectancy theory in 1964. In it, he proposed the idea that people are influenced by the expected results of their actions. The behaviours that an individual engages in depends on what they believe they will gain from doing them. In his theory, Vroom examines how individuals choose between alternative behaviours; this is the process through which outcomes become desirable and are pursued. The premise, or underlying belief, of the theory is that a person's level of motivation depends on how much they want something and how likely they are to get it.

The Expectancy theory focuses on the following three relationships:

1. **Effort to performance expectancy** – The effort or motivational force that individuals will put into pursuing a particular course of action, which is based on the perceived probability that a given amount of effort will affect their performance.
2. **Performance to outcome expectancy** – The degree to which individuals perceive performing at a certain level will result in the achievement of expected outcomes.
3. **Outcomes and valences** – The extent to which the rewards provided by the organisation satisfy an individual's needs and goals and the degree of attractiveness and importance of those rewards for the individual. An *outcome* is that which results from performance and may include pay, benefits, promotion, recognition, stress and reduction in time with family and friends. *Valence* refers to the attractiveness or unattractiveness, in other words the value, of a particular outcome to the individual. A positive valance is generally attached to outcomes such as pay and benefits, whereas a negative valance is attached to the experience of stress and a reduction of free time.

Vroom proposed that for motivation to occur the person must expect that there will be more positive than negative outcomes resulting from their performance. This in turn causes the individual to exert effort, which affects their level of performance. Therefore, the relationship between effort, performance and outcomes is demonstrated.

Porter and Lawler (1968) extended the Expectancy theory by proposing that performance results in both intrinsic and extrinsic rewards. *Intrinsic* factors exist within the person and include a sense of accomplishment and achievement. *Extrinsic* factors, which are tangible and easier to identify and measure, include pay, benefits and promotional opportunities. Porter and Lawler asserted that individuals engage in a social comparison process to determine the equity of the rewards they have received. Their equity perception impacts on the level of satisfaction experienced, which affects future effort and performance.

Vroom's Expectancy theory underlines the *individual nature of motivation* and the fact that there is no one universally appropriate means of motivating people. Managers need to acquire an understanding of the individual needs and expectations of each employee. By providing a means of influencing expectatations, a manager can have a significant influence on the performance of employees.

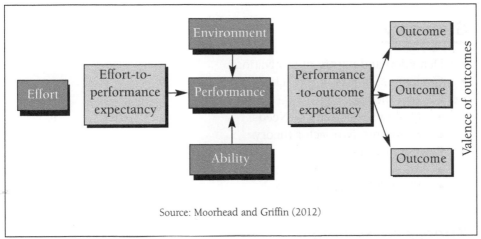

Source: Moorhead and Griffin (2012)

Figure 7.7 Vroom's Expectancy theory of motivation

No one single answer exists about how to motivate people at work. However, collectively, the content and process approaches provide a framework for understanding what people want from the workplace and how they can achieve their goals. The relevance of these different theories relates directly to the particular work situation in which they are applied.

7.5 Conclusion

Motivation arises from the relationship between needs, behaviour aimed at the fulfilment of needs and the achievement of goals. The content theorists attempted to describe human needs. Maslow arranged needs in a hierarchy of importance from physiological, to security, to belongingness, to esteem, to self-actualisation at the highest level. Herzberg provided an understanding of motivation in the workplace. He identified the factors leading to feelings of job dissatisfaction and job satisfaction, which impact on an employee's level of motivation. The process theorists examined how people choose between certain behavioural options in order to satisfy their needs. Adams investigated the response made by individuals to the experience of equity and inequity in the workplace. Vroom provided an insight into how expectations influence the effort and subsequent performance of employees. A motivated workforce is essential to the success of all organisations. Motivated workers achieve more and have a more positive experience in the workplace. An understanding of the theories of motivation provides an insight and support to practising managers. Catlette and Hadden (2001), in their book entitled *Contented Cows Give Better Milk*, remind us that 'motivated people move faster'.

Summary

- Definition and nature of motivation.
- Content vs. process approaches.
- Content theories:
  - Maslow's Hierarchy of Needs.
  - Herzberg's Two-factor theory.
- Process theories:
  - Adams' Equity theory.
  - Vroom's Expectancy theory.

Theory to real life

1. Think about a time when your level of performance was influenced directly by your level of motivation.
2. How do you satisfy the needs identified by Maslow on the hierarchy?
3. Consider the times in your life that you have experienced inequity. What response did you make to the perceived inequity?
4. What do you expect to achieve from your current course? How have your expectations influenced your effort and performance to date?

Exercises

1. Divide the class into two groups. Group 1 should think about the experience of being unmotivated in the workplace and consider how this would impact on how employees think, feel and are likely to behave. Group 2 should think about the experience of being motivated in the workplace and consider how this would impact on how employees think, feel and are likely to behave. Group 1 and Group 2 should present their findings.

2. Based on Herzberg's Two-factor theory of motivation, provide advice for a manager about how to reduce feelings of job dissatisfaction and increase feelings of job satisfaction in the workplace.
3. Think of a job that you do now or one that you have done in the past. Describe two ways that your job could be redesigned so that you and other employees would be motivated to perform at a higher level.
4. In groups of four or five, discuss the role that money plays in motivating people at work, making reference to the theories of motivation.

Essay questions

1. Define motivation and describe the need for managers to understand the concept of motivation.
2. Identify the central differences between the content and process approaches to motivation.
3. Evaluate the relevance of Maslow's theory of basic human needs for managers in organisations.
4. Examine Herzberg's Two-factor theory of motivation and describe how a manager could use this information to motivate employees.
5. Describe the importance of equity in the workplace, with reference to Adams' Equity theory.
6. Review Vroom's Expectancy theory of motivation.
7. 'A process and a content theory of motivation are not mutually exclusive approaches to human motivation. They each have something to contribute to our understanding of why people do the things they do.' Provide an explanation of this statement, using one theory from each approach to illustrate your answer.

Short questions

1. Propose a definition of motivation.
2. Complete the following diagram of the process of motivation.

3. What is the difference between the content and process approaches to motivation?
4. Complete a diagram of Maslow's Hierarchy of Needs, inserting the needs at each level of the hierarchy.
5. What are the two factors identified by Herzberg in his theory of motivation?
6. How could a manager use Herzberg's Two-factor theory?
7. What is equity?
8. What responses do people make to perceived inequity in the workplace?
9. According to Vroom, on what does our motivation level depend?

8
LEADERSHIP

Objectives

This chapter will help you to:

* Propose a definition of leadership.
* Understand the essential differences between managers and leaders.
* Describe the trait approach to leaders.
* Examine the behavioural approach to leadership.
* Gain an insight into the contingency leadership models.
* Appreciate the factors contributing to successful leadership.

8.1 Leadership defined

Leadership is an essential factor in the success of any kind of social activity and in particular to organisational effectiveness. It is a complex activity that is influenced by many external factors. When a leader is successful, the activity appears all too often as effortless. However, leadership is influenced by many factors relating to the individual, the people around him or her and the environment.

Leaders exist in all the different environments that surround us, including our families and friends, in school and college, in political and religious life, in the mass media, in business and in the community.

Leaders have been written about as those who get others to follow and who get people to do things willingly. Leadership is associated with factors such as motivation, communication, delegation, empowerment and teamwork.

According to Buchanan and Huczynski (2010), leadership is '**the process of influencing the activities of an organized group in its efforts toward goal setting and goal achievement**'.

Leadership is '**the process of directing and influencing the task-related activities of group members**' (Stoner and Freeman, 1992).

Jago (1982) states that '**leadership is both a process and a property**'. As a *process,* it is the use of non-coercive influence to direct and co-ordinate the activities of those who belong to a group to achieve a goal. As a *property,* it is the set of characteristics ascribed to those who are seen to use such influence successfully.

Leaders have the ability to *influence* a group to achieve a set of goals.

8.2 Management vs. leadership

The terms 'management' and 'leadership' are often used interchangeably as if there is no substantial difference between the activities. However, fundamental differences exist that distinguish leadership from management. According to Bennis and Nanus (1985), 'managers do things right' while 'leaders do the right things'.

Manager	Leader
Motivates people and administers resources to achieve stated organisational goals	Motivates people to develop new objectives
Short range view	Long-range perspective
A copy	An original
Maintains	Develops
Focuses on system and structure	Focuses on people
Implements	Shapes
Relies on control	Inspires trust
Eye on the botttom line	Eye on the horizon
Narrows down horizons	Opens up horizons
Rational	Emotional
Classic good soldier	Own person
Accepts the status quo	Challenges the status quo
Does the right thing	Does the right thing
Source: Adapted from Bennis (1989)	

Table 8.1 Distinguishing between a manager and a leader

Management is the ability to get things done through other people in order to achieve stated organisational goals. Management depends on a formal position of power. The orientation is towards short-term problem-solving and maintaining stability.

   Leadership arises from a social influence process; it does not involve force or coercion. It is important to note that a leader may have a formal or an informal position in any group or organisation. Mullins (1991) has described leadership as an 'inspirational process'. A leader is change-oriented and focuses on long-term strategy. This was highlighted by Bennis (1989) when he commented on the fact that 'leaders conquer the context – the volatile, turbulent, ambiguous surroundings that sometimes seem to conspire against us and will surely suffocate if we let them – while managers surrender to it'.

   Leadership and management can be understood as two complementary activities. In order for organisations to be effective they require strong management and strong leadership.

8.3 Theoretical approaches to leadership

A number of approaches have emerged that focus on different aspects of leadership, but collectively provide a good insight into the factors contributing to successful leadership.

Trait approach

This research commenced over one hundred years ago and persisted up to the 1950s. It attempted to describe the set of traits possessed by the effective leader. It was believed that leaders were born and not made; thus, the traits would be innate, stable and enduring. The objective was to identify the traits, measure them and then use them to select leaders. It is also termed the *Great Person theory of leadership*.

The traits identified include dominance, confidence and intelligence. Prominent theorists within this approach included Gibb (1947) and Stogdill (1948). The research produced long, subjective lists with little agreement about the central traits relating to effective leadership.

According to Judge *et al.* (2002), an understanding of the personality traits of leaders could be achieved using the Big Five personality framework (see Chapter 5). Their study of the leadership literature revealed that extroversion was the most important trait of effective leaders. However, the trait of extroversion has been shown to be more significantly linked to leader emergence than leader effectiveness. Other traits related to leadership are conscientiousness and openness to experience.

Studies indicate that effective leaders are emotionally intelligent (Goleman, 1995, 2000). Leaders who rate highly on emotional intelligence have the ability to identify, evaluate and manage their emotions and the emotions of others and of groups. People have different levels of emotional intelligence, which provides them with a variety and level of skills. These skills include the ability to manage relationships, to communicate effectively, to resolve conflict, to be self-aware, to have empathy and to motivate and inspire. Emotional intelligence has been identified as a significant factor in the workplace, influencing productivity, efficiency and teamwork, but further investigation is required.

Behavioural approach

The behavioural approach aimed to uncover the set of behaviours displayed by the effective leader. The behaviours of effective leaders were believed to differ from the behaviours of ineffective leaders. Leadership was understood to be an observable activity. The belief was held that if specific leadership behaviour could be identified then the possibility of teaching leadership may exist. The research started in the late 1940s and early 1950s.

The theories that exist within this approach include:

- The Michigan Studies
- The Ohio State Studies
- The Managerial Grid.

The Michigan Studies

This research was undertaken by Rensis Likert (1961) to distinguish the pattern of leadership behaviour that results in effective group performance. Interviews were conducted at the University of Michigan with supervisors and subordinates of high- and low-productivity groups to examine leader behaviour. The results revealed two types of leader behaviour:

1. **Job-centred leader behaviour** – This type of leader pays close attention to the work of employees, explains work procedures and is mainly interested in the efficient completion of tasks.
2. **Employee-centred leader behaviour** – This type of leader builds effective work groups and is concerned with the human aspects of the group.

Employee-centred leaders were found to achieve higher levels of both group productivity and job satisfaction. Whereas job-centred leaders were associated with lower levels of group productivity and job satisfaction.

According to Likert, the leader demonstrates either job-centred leader behaviour or employee-centred leader behaviour.

The Ohio State Studies

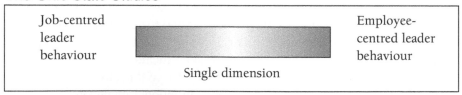

Figure 8.1 The Michigan Studies

This theory was proposed by Fleishman *et al.* (1955). They developed a questionnaire with over a thousand items and distributed it to military and industrial environments. The aim of the research was to assess the perception of leader behaviour. Two forms of leader behaviour emerged:

1. **Consideration behaviour** – The leader is concerned with the feelings of others, respects their ideas, shows mutual trust, has regard for subordinates and engages in two-way communication.

2. **Initiating structure behaviour** – The roles of the leader and the subordinate are clearly defined. The leader tells people what is expected of them and their status may be reinforced by use of jargon, wearing uniforms that identify rank, having separate canteens and washrooms and other privileges such as on-site parking.

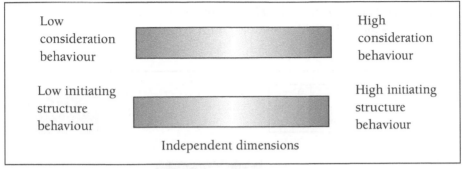

Figure 8.2 The Ohio State Studies

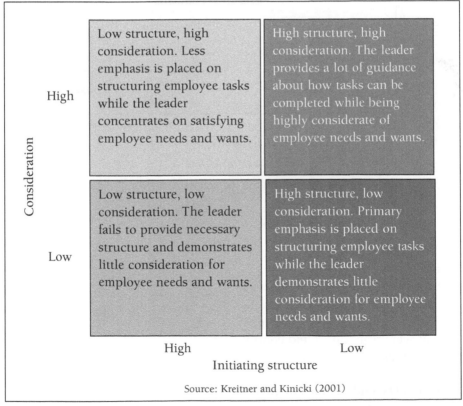

Figure 8.3 Four leadership styles derived from the Ohio State Studies

The Managerial Grid

Blake and Mouton (1964) provided a framework for understanding and applying effective leadership. They believed that the role of the manager is to foster attitudes about behaviour that promote performance, creativity and entrepreneurship. Leadership can be taught and learned. Blake and Mouton uncovered a number of different types of supervision which combine different levels of *concern for people* and *concern for production*.

The **Managerial Grid** identifies numerous types of possible leader behaviour.

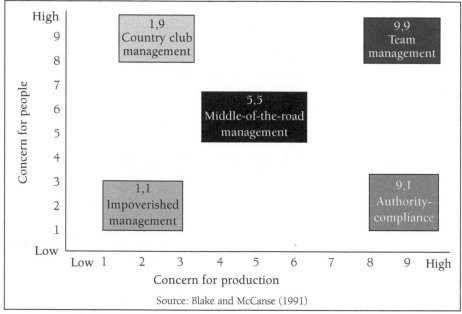

Figure 8.4 Leadership behaviour in the Managerial Grid

9,1 Authority-compliance style:

- Task management.
- Production issues.
- Schedules met in methodical way.
- Disagreement is dysfunctional.
- People are resources to be used.
- Managers plan, direct and control.
- Viewed as drivers of staff.

1,9 Country club management style:

- People concerns.

- Support and encouragement.
- Create harmony and avoid conflict.
- Regarded as one of the workers.
- Create comfortable working environment.
- 'Good fellowship'.

1,1 Impoverished management style:

- Little concern for production or people.
- Avoids responsibility and commitment.
- Avoids contact; appears remote.
- Believes people are lazy.
- Conflict is inevitable.

5,5 Middle-of-the-road style:

- Acceptable levels of production.
- Concern for people.
- Firm but fair attitude.
- Tries to keep everyone happy.
- Confidence in subordinates.

9,9 Team management style:

- High concern for people.
- Goal is integration.
- Highest standards.
- Best results for all.
- Involvement and participation.
- Goals and their achievement is a fulfilling challenge.
- Conflict is handled in an open, not personal manner.
- Long-term development and trust.
- Organisation culture needs to support this type of leader.

The application of the various leadership styles identified by Blake and Mouton has implications for the leaders themselves, the employees and the organisation.

The behavioural theories have provided an insight into the behaviours that contribute to leader effectiveness, but consideration needs to be given to situational factors.

Contingency approach

The earlier approaches to leadership attempted to identify a universal 'one best style' approach. However, these did not take into account the fact that the prediction of leadership success is complex.

Situational variables relating to the personal characteristics of employees and to the environment have a strong influence in explaining leadership success. The contingency theorists aimed to identify key situational variables that made one style of leadership more relevant than others in particular circumstances.

MATCH :	Leadership style + Conditions

The LPC theory of leadership

The **least preferred co-worker (LPC) theory** of leadership was developed by Fred E. Fiedler (1967). His belief was that the relative effectiveness of a leader is determined by how favourable the situation is for the leader. Fiedler's main concern was to effectively match the leader and the situation.

Fiedler first assessed the basic personality traits of the leader and secondly examined the elements of the situation. This approach enabled him to examine the effectiveness of the match between the leader and the situation.

In order to determine whether a leader is task- or relationship-motivated, Fiedler used a questionnaire. This was called the LPC (least preferred co-worker) scale. A high score indicates that the person is relationship- oriented and a low score that they are task-oriented.

Think of the person with whom you work least well. He/she may be someone you work with now, or someone you knew in the past. He/she does not have to be the person you like least well, but should be the person with whom you now have or have had the most difficulty in getting a job done. Describe this person as he/she appears to you by placing an 'x' at the point at which you believe best describes that person. Do this for each pair of adjectives.

Pleasant	8	7	6	5	4	3	2	1	Unpleasant
Friendly	8	7	6	5	4	3	2	1	Unfriendly
Rejecting	8	7	6	5	4	3	2	1	Accepting
Helpful	8	7	6	5	4	3	2	1	Frustrating
Unenthusiastic	8	7	6	5	4	3	2	1	Enthusiastic
Tense	8	7	6	5	4	3	2	1	Relaxed
Distant	8	7	6	5	4	3	2	1	Close
Cold	8	7	6	5	4	3	2	1	Warm
Co-operative	8	7	6	5	4	3	2	1	Unco-operative
Supportive	8	7	6	5	4	3	2	1	Hostile
Boring	8	7	6	5	4	3	2	1	Interesting
Quarrelsome	8	7	6	5	4	3	2	1	Harmonious
Self-assured	8	7	6	5	4	3	2	1	Hesitant
Efficient	8	7	6	5	4	3	2	1	Inefficient
Gloomy	8	7	6	5	4	3	2	1	Cheerful
Open	8	7	6	5	4	3	2	1	Guarded

Scoring: Your score on the LPC scale is a measure of your leadership style and it indicates your primary motivation in a work setting. To determine your score, add up the points (1 to 8) for each of the 16 items. If your score is 64 or above, you are a high LPC person or relationship-oriented. If your score is 57 or below, you are a low LPC person or task-oriented. If your score falls between 58 and 63, you will need to determine for yourself in which category you belong.

Source: Fiedler and Chemers (1974)

Table 8.2 LPC activity

Fiedler investigated the elements of the situation that determine how favourable it is for the leader. He believed that three factors should be considered:

1. **Leader—member relations** – The relationship between the leader and employees is evaluated as either being good or poor. When relations are good there is trust, respect, acceptance and confidence.
2. **Task structure** – This is rated as *high* or *low*. When there is high task structure, it is easy for the leader to determine what should be done, by whom and for what purpose. It concerns the degree to which tasks are clearly defined and the extent to which they can be completed by following detailed instructions or standard procedures. Typical jobs in fast food restaurants have high task structure.
3. **Position power of the leader** – The leader either has a strong or weak position of power, which involves the level of authority to assign work, reward and punish and recommend employees for promotion.

Table 8.3 identifies the leadership approach that is believed to achieve a high level of group performance in each of the eight situations identified.

Situational control	High control situations			Moderate control situations			Low control situations	
Leader–member relations	Good	Good	Good	Good	Poor	Poor	Poor	Poor
Task structure	High	High	High	Low	High	High	Low	Low
Position power	Strong	Weak	Strong	Weak	Strong	Strong	Strong	Weak
Situation	I	II	III	IV	V	VI	VII	VIII
Optimal leadership style	Task-motivated leadership			Relationship-motivated leadership Source: Fiedler (1967)			Task-motivated leadership	

Table 8.3 Fiedler's contingency model

The most favourable situation for a leader is when leader—member relations are good, the task structure is high and the position of power is strong. The least favourable situation is when poor leader—member relations exist, there is low task structure and the leader has a weak position of power.

The mismatched leader cannot easily adapt to the situation and achieve high levels of performance. It is important to an organisation that leaders are placed in a situation that matches their task and relationship orientation. If a person's style does not match the situation there are two choices, either the leader can be removed and a new one appointed or the situation must be changed. Fiedler (1967) advocated 'engineering the job to fit the manager'.

The Path-Goal theory of leadership

Presented by House (1971), this theory also states that leadership effectiveness depends on the correct match between the leader and the situation. House proposes that leaders can adapt their style to suit different situations. The theory is based on Vroom's Expectancy theory of motivation and therefore the fundamental belief is that people are motivated by how much they want something and how likely they are to get it. The behaviour of leaders influences the expectations of employees as to the extent of the rewards available for task completion. It is very important for a boss to understand what an employee wants and expects from work and the nature of their values in order to gain an insight into their attitudes and behaviours. A leader must understand what motivates employees in order to influence their behaviour and achieve high levels of performance.

The leader affects employee performance by clarifying the required behaviour = PATHS. By ensuring the employee follows the correct path, the leader can help them to achieve the desired rewards = GOALS. The theory is therefore called the **Path-Goal theory.**

In order to influence employee attitudes and behaviour, the leader must match their style to the situation. House identified four leadership behaviours:

1. **Directive leadership** – The leader clearly tells subordinates what has to be done. The guidance provided is specific and definitive standards are communicated.
2. **Supportive leadership** – The approach is friendly, there is concern for the well-being of employees and that their needs are being met.
3. **Participative leadership** – Employees are consulted and involved in the decision-making process.
4. **Achievement-oriented leadership** – The highest standards are aimed for by the leader and goals are seen as a fulfilling challenge. Confidence is shown in subordinates.

The behaviours displayed by leaders will change depending on the situation. Two situational factors have been identified by House:

1. **Personal characteristics of subordinates:**
   - **Locus of control** – People either have an internal or external centre of control. Those who have an internal locus of control believe that what happens to them is caused by them and favour a participative leader. Those who have an external locus of control believe that events that occur are caused by forces outside of them and favour a directive leader.

- **Perceived ability** – Those who rate their ability highly do not highly rate directive leadership and prefer participative and achievement-oriented leadership, whereas those who do not rate their ability highly prefer directive leadership.
2. **Characteristics of the environment** – These include task structure, the formal authority system and the primary work group. The leader will motivate subordinates to the extent that they help subordinates deal with uncertainty in the environment.

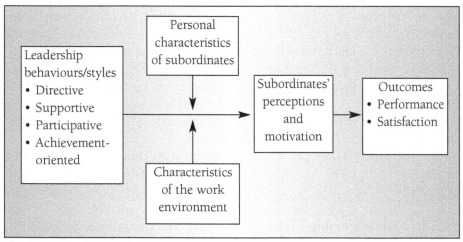

Figure 8.5 Path-Goal theory

The Path-Goal theory of leadership emphasises the importance of the leader adapting their style to fit the situation. The correct match betweeen the leader and the conditions that are present in the organisation at the time will contribute to the successsful operation of the organisation.

8.4 Conclusion

Leaders influence the behaviour of employees in order to achieve organisational goals. The trait theories identified the traits and characteristics that differentiate effective leaders from ineffective leaders. The behavioural approach examined the behaviours displayed by leaders in terms of their job and employee orientation. The contingency approach attempted to provide a framework to emphasise the importance of matching the style of the leader to the situation. The academic research into leadership is ongoing and the need for effective leadership in organisations is ever present. The challenges for both researchers and practitioners include the areas of ethical leadership, management of diversity, teamwork, strategic leadership, creativity and learning, leaders as change agents, emotional intelligence, effective communication and creating a culture of collaboration.

Summary

- Leadership defined.
- Management vs. leadership.
- Theoretical approaches to leadership:
  - Trait approach
  - Behavioural approach
  - Contingency approach.

Theory to real life

1. Identify leaders in business, politics, religion, sport, fashion and music.
2. Think about three people who have acted as leaders in your life.
3. Name three organisations that have effective leaders.
4. Describe how managers and leaders affect the performance of an organisation you are familiar with.
5. Name some of the challenges that leaders face today.
6. In your opinion, how important is it that a leader's style is adaptable and why?

Exercises

1. What is the most important ability that a leader must possess?
2. Review the functions of managers and make a brief presentation to your class/tutorial group on the key concerns of managers.
3. Examine the functions of leaders and make a brief presentation to your class/tutorial group on the central characteristics of leaders.
4. Describe the traits that you believe effective leaders have.
5. In class, divide into two groups and debate the following statement: 'The best leaders encourage participation from their subordinates'. One group should be for the motion and the other against the motion.

Essay questions

1. Examine the differences and similarities between the concepts of management and leadership.
2. Consider how the behavioural theories have attempted to explain leadership in an organisational setting.
3. Examine the approach to leadership adopted by Blake and Mouton in the Managerial Grid.
4. a. Propose a definition of leadership.
   b. Evaluate Fiedler's contingency theory of leadership.
5. Investigate the leader behaviours and situational factors included in the Path-Goal theory of leadership.

Short questions

1. Propose a definition of leadership.
2. According to Bennis and Nanus, what is the main difference between managers and leaders?
3. What was the aim of the trait approach to leadership?
4. What did the behavioural approach to leadership attempt to identify?
5. Name three theories of leadership that are part of the behavioural approach.
6. What is initiating structure behaviour?
7. What is the aim of the contingency approach to leadership?
8. Fiedler stated that a leader's style is either _____ or_____ -oriented.
9. Name the four styles of leadership included in the Path-Goal theory.

9
GROUPS AND TEAMS

Objectives

This chapter will help you to:

- Propose a definition of a group.
- Identify the reasons for group formation.
- Describe the difference between a formal and informal group.
- Understand the stages of group development.
- Examine important factors influencing group performance.
- Appreciate the benefits of teamworking.

9.1 Group dynamics defined

People are social beings and have a primary need for relationships. Organisations are social systems and relationships are of fundamental importance to the effective functioning of organisations.

Group dynamics is the study of people in groups and also a general term used for group processes. In psychology and sociology, a group is two or more individuals who are associated with each other through social relationships. As a result of the fact that people in groups interact with and influence one another, groups develop a number of dynamic processes that separate them from a random collection of individuals. These group processes include norms, roles, development, need fulfilment, social influence and effects on behaviour. The main focus of the field of group dynamics is primarily concerned with small group behaviour.

> **A psychological group is any number of people who (a) interact with each other, (b) are psychologically aware of each other, and (c) perceive themselves to be a group** (Schein, 1988).

> **A group is two or more persons who interact with one another in such a manner that each person influences and is influenced by each other person** (Shaw, 1991).

The concept of interaction is central to the definition of a group. If people do not communicate with each other, they will not be able to share knowledge, beliefs or feelings and therefore will not influence each other. Those who interact with one another through face-to-face meetings, phone calls, e-mail and through many other channels of communication will exchange information and have an effect on each others' thoughts, feelings and behaviour. Interaction will lead to the development of the group; the quality of the interaction will depend on the type of group.

A group is characterised by its degree of communication, cohesiveness and conformity. First, members of a group interact with each other, the extent of face-to-face communication and the use of other methods of communication being determined by the size of the group. Secondly, the level of cohesiveness is determined by the extent to which members of a group exhibit solidarity and share common attitudes, values and beliefs. High levels of cohesiveness lead to co-operation between members and the achievement of goals. Finally, people in groups tend to give in or conform to standards of behaviour or norms, which include dress codes, expression of particular attitudes and behaviours. Sanctions are imposed if members do not adhere to norms. The ultimate sanction is rejection from the group.

9.2 Reasons for group formation

Individuals are motivated to join groups as groups provide a means by which needs can be fulfilled. People are resistant to leaving groups since this would frustrate their ability to meet needs. The reasons for group formation include:

- **Interpersonal attraction** – Individuals are attracted to those that are similar to themselves. Group members usually have one or more factors in common, such as living in the same area, working in the same profession, having the same educational background or work experience, having the same interests, hobbies, values and even sharing the same personality traits and attitudes.
- **Group's activities and goals** – Individuals join groups because they enjoy the activity of the group. This may be a sporting, political, religious or professional activity. People also join groups because they believe in and support the goal of the group. This may mean that they contribute their time, effort and even money to achieve an objective they believe in, such as charity work.
- **Social affiliation** – People are social animals and need human companionship. They therefore seek out others to spend time with and complete tasks. The extent to which individuals are driven towards others is influenced to a great extent by whether they have an extroverted or introverted personality type.

- **Security** – When people are with others, it provides them with a feeling that there is safety and protection in numbers and meets their need for security.
- **Esteem** – Group membership can fulfil an individual's need for esteem and enhance feelings of self-worth and value. This can be achieved by becoming part of a group that is perceived to be high status and also by receiving recognition and praise from other group members.
- **Power** – Groups provide a means to influence how other people think, feel and behave. Groups provide a strong powerbase, as is demonstrated in the saying 'united we stand, divided we fall'. In addition, groups afford opportunities for members to achieve both formal and informal positions of power.
- **Identity** – People are constantly seeking to answer the question 'Who am I?' Groups provide people with an understanding about themselves, which is clearly seen through an individual's curriculum vitae. The information contained on a person's CV associates them with a range of different groups, such as community, school, college, work and sports groups. The person defines themselves by the groups that they have belonged to in the past or that they are currently part of and even the groups that they aspire to join.
- **Accomplishment** – More than one individual is normally required to accomplish a task. Through group membership, a person can achieve much more than they can on their own.

9.3 Types of groups

Groups in the workplace can either be formal or informal. Different types of groups serve various functions and satisfy different needs for individuals.

Formal groups

Formal groups are types of groups deliberately created to perform a specific work-related task. Formal groups are made up of *command,* or *functional, groups* and *task groups.* Command, or functional, groups are relatively permanent and are included in the organisational structure. They include the groups that make up the departments in the organisation, such as finance, human resources and marketing. People are commanded to undertake a particular job within a functional area. Task groups are more temporary by nature and are used to undertake a project or solve a particular problem. Members of a task group are usually members of a command, or functional, group within the organisation. A task group may be used to brainstorm ideas for a new product or service or to examine methods for introducing change.

The group may consist of members from a number of departments within the organisation. When ideas have been generated or problems resolved, members return to their command, or functional, group.

Informal groups

The social needs of individuals drive them to form informal groups, which consist of friendship and interest groups. Friendship groups are relatively permanent, while interest groups tend to be more temporary in nature. People may join a group to undertake a hobby or sporting interest but in time may move on to something else.

An insight into the behaviour of employees in the workplace is achieved by gaining knowledge about the type of formal and informal groups of which people are members. Groups have a very strong motivational influence on people's behaviour and their influence should not be underestimated.

9.4 Stages of group development

Groups are not static, but dynamic. They form, develop, mature and disband. It is not until a group is mature that it is fully efficient and effective. The four stages of group development were first described in 1965 by Bruce W. Tuckman, a respected educational psychologist. Having examined the behaviour of small groups in a variety of settings, Tuckman identified the distinct phases they go through. He proposed that groups need to experience all four stages of development before they achieve maximum effectiveness. The model was further developed in 1977 in conjunction with May Ann Jensen, and a fifth stage was added.

Tuckman and Jensen described the distinct stages that a group experiences as it comes together and starts to operate. This process can occur subconsciously, although an understanding of the stages can be of great benefit to a group in reaching effectiveness more quickly.

Forming

Individual behaviour is driven by a desire to be accepted by others and to avoid controversy or conflict. Members share background information about themselves, but serious issues and feelings are avoided. Individuals are gathering information and impressions about each other and about the scope of the task and how to approach it. Even though individuals may experience some anxiety about joining a new group, this is a comfortable stage to be in.

If members know each other already, this will be a brief stage. It has also been referred to as the stage of *mutual acceptance.*

Storming

As members get to know one another and are more secure and self-assured, they begin to discuss feelings and opinions openly. Issues for consideration may relate to the work of the group itself or to roles and responsibilities within the group. Some members will be pleased to be getting into the work of the group, while others will long for the comfort and security of the previous stage. This stage is characterised by conflict and may be uncomfortable for some members. Members begin to identify what they want individually and from the group as a whole. The culture of the organisation and individuals will influence the degree to which conflict, and hostility are demonstrated or suppressed. To manage the conflict, individuals will search for structural clarity and rules to prevent the occurrence of ongoing conflict. This stage is also termed *the communication stage.*

Norming

Members of the group begin to develop ways of working together. A sense of identity, unity and purpose begins to emerge. The 'rules of engagement' or norms for the group become established and the scope of the group's tasks and responsibilities becomes clear and is agreed on. Norms can be defined as a regular pattern of thinking or behaving that a group has adopted. The orientation of members changes from one that related to each of them as individuals to one that is focused on the needs of the group. People start to appreciate each other's skills and experience. Members listen to one another, appreciate and support each other and are prepared to change established views. The feeling is one of a cohesive and effective work group. The goals of the group have been agreed upon, the roles and tasks assigned and standards are set. A disadvantage of the norming stage is that members may begin to fear the inevitable future break-up of the group and resist change of any sort. Overall, a framework for action has been developed and the group has progressed through the *decision-making stage.*

Performing

At this stage, an effective group structure has been established and is characterised by a state of interdependence and flexibility. Members get on with the task at hand and achieve goals. They know each other sufficiently well to work together and to trust each other to undertake independent activity. People undertake activities that benefit the group and make changes in roles and responsibilities as needed. This mature group constantly evaluates activities and takes corrective action. This stage is characterised by flexibility, spontaneity and self-correction. Loyalty, morale and group identity are at high levels, which focuses the energy of the group on task accomplishment. High levels of motivation of productivity are demonstrated, coupled with control and organisation of activities.

Adjourning

This final stage concerns the completion of tasks and the disengagement of members from the activities and from group members. At this point, the orientation moves away from the task and towards the individual. People will feel proud of their achievements and satisfied with having been part of an effective group. They are effectively drawing a line in the sand by recognising what they have achieved and moving on. Some have described this stage as *deforming and mourning* to recognise the sense of loss experienced by individuals.

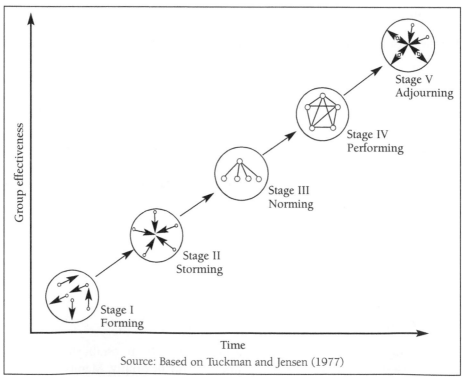

Source: Based on Tuckman and Jensen (1977)

Figure 9.1 Tuckman and Jensen's theory of the stages of group development

Tuckman and Jensen's theory is valuable because:

• It can help to explain some of the problems of group working.
• The theory provides an understanding of the fact that some groups may experience problems at an early stage that may not have been addressed and that may have a negative impact on group performance.
• It recognises that a group may become stuck at one stage, which will govern their attitudes and behaviour towards each other and the task.
• It shows that interventions may need to be introduced because groups may need to re-experience one or more stages of development to maintain cohesiveness and productivity. This could be done through formal training on or off the job or through a social or sports activity.
• It acknowledges that groups are dynamic and are constantly forming and changing as new members join, others leave and as adjustments are made to work-related activities.

The effective management of people in groups presents a continuing challenge for management. This model provides a framework for understanding the nature of group development and demonstrates the benefits of creating a mature work group for both the individual group members and the organisation.

9.5 Group performance factors

The performance of a group in an organisation is influenced by the reasons for the group formation, the stage of its development and other significant factors including size, composition, norms and cohesiveness.

Size

Groups can be divided arbitrarily into being either small or large. The appropriate size of the group will be determined by the type of activity that is being undertaken. A small group has the benefit that it allows for the frequent interaction of members and the free exchange of information. It is also easier and quicker to reach decisions with a small group of people. Small groups often arise out of larger groups in organisations, which can provide advantages and disadvantages. Advantages include the social support that a small group offers and opportunities for increased involvement and participation in decision-making. The disadvantage with small groups is that cliques may form and create 'in group, out group' scenarios, resulting in feelings of isolation for those who are not part of a particular group. Different groups may develop contrasting patterns of working and conflict may arise between cliques.

Large groups have a wide range of resources available to them and are capable of completing a number of different tasks. A large group enables individuals to satisfy a number of needs, including power, identity, security and accomplishment. The interactions between members of a large group are formalised and considerable time is spent on administrative activities. A negative aspect of large groups is that people may find them intimidating and this may inhibit participation. Absenteeism can also be an issue with large groups when members may not feel a great sense of individual importance and may not believe that their output will be directly related to their performance in the workplace. This may result in a person experiencing a diminished sense of responsibility in a large group.

Social loafing is a tendency for group members to exert less effort in a large group than they would working alone. It frequently results from the assumption by some employees that if they do not work hard other members will do the work anyway. In addition, employees may perceive that other group members are not contributing their fair share, so they reduce their input in an attempt to experience equity. Finally, it may be because the task is seen as unimportant or boring.

According to George (1992), social loafing can be reversed or prevented by taking the following actions:

- Keep group sizes small and redefine roles so free riders are more visible and peer pressure becomes more likely to occur.
- Increase accountability by making performance expectations clear and specific.
- Make rewards dependent on an employee's performance contributions.

In conclusion, the most effective size of the group is determined by the task to be undertaken and the ability of group members to interact and influence each other effectively.

Composition

A group can be constituted of members who are either similar or different in the factors relating to the completion of work-related activities.

- **Homogeneity** – A **homogeneous group** consists of members similar to each other in one or more ways that is central to the completion of tasks. Similarities may exist between members in relation to their qualifications, experience and skill. This type of group is effective at completing simple tasks, sequential activities and those that require speed and co-operation. Due to the commonalities between members, there is less conflict and more interaction.

* **Heterogeneity** – A **heterogeneous group** is made up of members who are different in one or more ways that is essential to the work of the group. The range of qualifications, experience and skills presented by this type of group enables the members to complete complex tasks. Heterogeneous groups work collectively to undertake tasks and are effective when creativity is required. Members provide a complex analysis of the task, but due to their diversity it may take longer to complete tasks.

Norms

A norm is a standard against which the appropriateness of a behaviour is judged. Norms represent the expected behaviours in a particular situation; they help members to understand what is expected of them in a certain situation and to predict how others may behave. Without norms, organisational life would be chaotic. Conflict can be seen to occur when norms are not adhered to, including those relating to punctuality, work rate and dress code. This conflict may result in verbal abuse, physical threats, ostracism and even rejection.

Norms result from the personality characteristics of members, the situation, the task and the traditions of the group. Norms serve a number of different functions. First, they help the group to survive by rejecting deviant behaviour that might undermine or threaten the existence of the group. Secondly, norms simplify and make behaviour within the group predictable, which increases productivity and enhances goal achievement. Thirdly, they provide the valuable purpose of helping members to avoid embarrassment by knowing the appropriate way to behave and therefore maintaining their self-esteem. Finally, the expression of the central values of the group can be achieved through norms. Values are held by work, political, religious and sporting organisations among many others and may be witnessed through their attitudes, culture and behaviours.

Cohesivesness

According to Festinger (1950), **cohesiveness** results from '**all forces acting on members to remain in the group**'. These forces include attraction to the group, resistance to leaving the group and overall motivation to remain a member because the group satisfies many needs for the individual. Cohesiveness is the extent to which a group is committed to staying together. This level of commitment can be increased by factors such as competition, external threats and success. Failure has a negative impact on cohesiveness.

Factors that increase group cohesiveness	Factors that decrease group cohesiveness
Agreement on group goals	Disagreement on goals
Frequency of interaction	Large group size
Personal attractiveness	Unpleasant experiences
Inter-group competition	Intra-group competition
Favourable evaluation	Domination by one or more members
Source: Szilagyi and Wallace (1990)	

Table 9.1 Factors affecting group cohesiveness

Cohesiveness is influenced by the maturity of the group, the degree of homogeneity of members, the size of the group and the frequency of interactions. Unity and solidarity are important characteristics of an effective work group; however, too high a level of cohesiveness can produce '*groupthink*'. Janis (1972) identified the fact that group members can become so close that disagreement between people becomes less and less likely to take place. As a consequence, the group develops a way of thinking that prevents them from being realistic or critical about what they are doing or how they are doing it. The members are less likely to question the reasons for undertaking tasks in a particular manner. When groupthink occurs, members become blind to weaknesses, believe that agreement is all-important and experience a false sense of security.

1. Leaders should assign the role of critical evaluator to every group member.

2. Leaders should not state their preferences at the beginning of a meeting.

3. Assign subgroups to independently develop proposals.

4. Periodically have outside experts review the group's deliberations. Invite them to sit in on some meetings.

5. During important deliberations, assign one member of the group to play the role of devil's advocate.

6. After formulating a tentative proposal, hold a second-chance meeting. Invite all members to express any residual doubts.

Source: Janis (1972)

Table 9.2 Remedies for groupthink

To fully understand the factors influencing the performance of any group, a study should be undertaken of the reasons for group formation, the stage of its development and performance factors including size, composition, norms and cohesiveness.

9.6 Teams

Teams have been defined as '**a small group of people with complimentary skills who work together to achieve a common purpose for which they hold themselves collectively accountable**' (Schermerhorn *et al.*, 1996). Effective and efficient teamwork goes beyond individual accomplishments, with the most effective teamwork being produced when all the individuals involved harmonise their contributions and work towards a common goal. Teamwork is about creating a work culture that values collaboration. People understand and believe that thinking, planning, decisions and actions are better when done co-operatively in a teamwork environment. People acknowledge and assimilate the belief that 'none of us is as good as all of us'.

West and Markiewicz (2004) contend that team-based working provides a number of benefits for organisations. These benefits include efficient processes; flexible response to change; improved effectiveness; reduced costs; increased innovation; effective partnering; customer involvement; employee commitment and well-being; and skill utilisation.

In addition, teamwork has the benefit of enhancing individual motivation, job satisfaction and self-esteem and increases the productivity and effectiveness of organisations. Belbin (1993) identified examples of different types of behaviour that led to distinct team contributions or team roles in organisations. He described a team role as 'a tendency to behave, contribute and interrelate with others in a particular way'. Belbin proposed that people display different team roles to varying degrees (see Figure 9.2). A balanced team will comprise a mixture of people who together display a range of team roles.

Teamwork can be used when:

- Better results are achieved working together.
- A mixture of talents and skills are required.
- Constant adjustment is needed in what employees do and how work is co-ordinated.
- Competition between individuals would be damaging for the organisation.
- The work environment produces too much stress for an individual to cope with alone.

Roles and descriptions – team role contribution	Allowable weaknesses
Plant Creative, imaginative, unorthodox. Solves difficult problems.	Ignores details. Too preoccupied to communicate effectively.
Resource investigator Extrovert, enthusiastic, communicative. Explores opportunities. Develops contacts.	Over-optimistic. Loses interest once initial enthusiasm has passed.
Co-ordinator Mature, confident, a good chairperson. Clarifies goals, promotes decision-making, delegates well.	Can be seen as manipulative. Delegates personal work.
Shaper Challenging, dynamic, thrives on pressure. Has the drive and courage to overcome obstacles.	Can provoke others. Hurts people's feelings.
Monitor–evaluator Sober, strategic and discerning. Sees all opinions. Judges accurately.	Lacks drive and ability to inspire others. Overly critical.
Teamworker Co-operative, mild, perceptive and diplomatic. Listens, builds, averts friction, calms the waters.	Indecisive in crunch situations. Can be easily influenced.
Implementer Disciplined, reliable, conservative and efficient. Turns ideas into practical actions.	Somewhat inflexible. Slow to respond to new possibilities.
Completer Painstaking, conscientious, anxious. Searches out errors and omissions. Delivers on time.	Inclined to worry unduly. Reluctant to delegate. Can be a nit-picker.
Specialist Single-minded, self-starting, dedicated. Provides knowledge and skills in rare supply.	Contributes on only a narrow front. Dwells on technicalities. Overlooks the 'big picture'.
Strength of contribution in any one of the roles is commonly associated with particular weaknesses. These are called allowable weaknesses. Executives are seldom strong in all nine team roles.	
Source: Belbin (1996)	

Table 9.3 Belbin's nine team roles

Signs of a good team:

- Informal, pleasant atmosphere
- Lots of discussions
- No resentment if ideas are modified or rejected
- Disagreements are confronted
- No hidden agendas
- Boss doesn't dominate the proceedings
- Nobody hogs the stage
- No one gets injured or ignored
- People are assigned tasks based on their capacity.

These are a few of the many quotes about the benefits of teamwork:

None of us is as smart as all of us.

Ken Blanchard

It is amazing how much you can accomplish when it doesn't matter who gets the credit.

Unknown

Teamwork: Simply stated, it is less 'me' and more 'we'.

Unknown

TEAM = Together Everyone Achieves More.

Unknown

The whole is greater than the sum of the parts.

Unknown

Teamwork is working together – even when apart.

Unknown

Coming together is a beginning.
Keeping together is progress.
Working together is success.

Henry Ford

A self-reinforcing upward spiral: performance stimulating pride stimulating performance.

Rosabeth Moss Kanter

9.7 Conclusion

A group consists of two or more people who interact, are psychologically aware of each other and have a collective identity. People are motivated to join groups to satisfy various needs, including security, affiliation and power. Formal and informal groups exist in organisations and influence the behaviour of employees. A group does not come into existence fully formed but develops through a number of stages. The performance of the group is affected by the success of its transition through each of the stages until the group reaches maturity. The performance of groups is dependent also on factors such as size, composition, norms and cohesiveness. The benefit of groups in organisations has been widely accepted and team-based working is a central issue for organisations today. It is critical that organisations develop and support effective teams. Teams provide a mixture of different knowledge, skills and abilities and offer the opportunity for learning, creativity and innovation.

Summary

- Nature of groups.
- Reasons for group formation.
- Types of groups.
- Stages of group development.
- Factors affecting group performance.
- Teamwork.

Theory to real life

1. Think about a group that you belong to at college or in work and reflect on the experience of each of the stages of development. What stage do you believe your group is at now? How does the stage of development influence the effectiveness of the group?
2. What norms have you noticed at home/college/work? What is the function of these norms? How are they enforced? How do they influence the type of behaviour displayed?
3. Consider the effect of group size on performance.
4. Provide examples from your own experience of when groupthink may have occurred.
5. To what extent are teams a feature of your normal life?
6. What are the benefits of teams in college/work/sports?

7. Based on the team roles identified by Belbin, what type of behaviour do you display? What are your strengths and weaknesses in a team?

Exercises

1. In class or during a tutorial, work in groups of four or five. The lecturer/tutor should provide each group with a supply of paper, paper clips and adhesive tape. Each group builds a paper tower with the materials supplied. The winning group is the one with the highest tower. One member should take notes that include contributions from all members about how the paper tower exercise is being undertaken and the role that each person is playing.

    These questions can be used by each group to reflect on the exercise and enhance learning.
    a. What tasks did the group undertake during the forming stage?
    b. How did the group go through the storming stage?
    c. What norms have been identified that influenced the work of the group?
    d. Is the group performing effectively? If not, what action needs to be taken?
    e. Were you an effective team? If so, why?
2. List the team roles identified by Belbin and consider their contribution to team effectiveness.
3. Prepare and make a presentation about the need for managers to have an understanding of the stages of group development in order to effectively manage the behaviour of groups and teams in the workplace.

Essay questions

1. Propose a definition of a group.
2. Describe the reasons why individuals join groups.
3. Explain the stages that groups go through from inception to maturity.
4. Investigate the impact that size, composition, norms and cohesiveness have on group performance.
5. Examine the nature of teams and the benefits of teamwork.

Short questions

1. A group has been defined as a number of people who _____ with each other.
2. In a psychological group each person influences and is influenced by each other person. TRUE/FALSE?
3. Name three reasons why people join groups.
4. Name the five stages of group development, according to Tuckman and Jensen.
5. What is a characteristic of a mature group?
6. In a homogeneous group, members are _____ in one or more ways that is critical to the work of the group.
7. In a heterogeneous group, members are _____ in one or more ways that is critical to the work of the group.
8. Name two problems that may occur in a large group.
9. What is social loafing?
10. What is a norm?
11. Name a benefit of having norms in an organisation.
12. Groupthink occurs when a group becomes so close that disagreement is unlikely. TRUE/FALSE?
13. Name four benefits of team-based working.
14. Name two signs of a good team.

10
CONFLICT IN ORGANISATIONS

Objectives

This chapter will help you to:

- Describe the nature of conflict in organisations.
- Identify the sources of conflict in the workplace.
- Understand the difference between functional and dysfunctional conflict.
- Describe the key perspectives on conflict.
- Propose methods of conflict resolution.

10.1 Nature of conflict in organisations

Conflict is an emotionally charged aspect of organisational behaviour. Conflict exists in all organisations and has many benefits, but excessive levels are undesirable. It is therefore important that an understanding of the nature of conflict exists and that interpersonal skills are developed to manage conflict effectively.

Conflict is a social process and involves more than one person or party. Conflict may involve individuals, groups, departments and organisations. Although conflict tends to be viewed as negative, irrational and fruitless, conflict can have strong positive dimensions, such as a way of articulating grievances and creating change, and can be perceived as rational and worthwhile.

According to Schermerhorn *et al.* (1985), conflict '**occurs whenever disagreement exists in a social situation over issues of substance or emotional discord**'.

Moorhead and Griffin (2012) define conflict as '**a process resulting in the perceptions of two parties that they are working in opposition to each other in ways that result in feelings of discomfort and/or animosity**'.

Interpersonal conflict can be described as a process that begins when one party *perceives* that another party has frustrated (or is about to frustrate) some concern of theirs. In the workplace, individuals may feel that another person is creating obstacles preventing the achievement of goals and, as a result, conflict takes place.

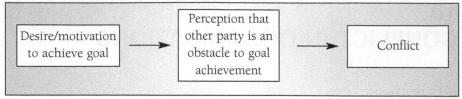

Figure 10.1 The process of conflict

Functional vs. dysfunctional conflict

Conflict in an organisation can be functional and provide many benefits to the organisation. However, conflict can also be dysfunctional and may damage the performance of an organisation. A lack of conflict in an organisation can indicate problems with group dynamics such as groupthink (Janis, 1972). An optimum level of conflict promotes motivation, innovation and change.

Functional conflict:

- Conflict is expected and is normal.
- Conflict benefits the individual, teams and the organisation and enhances performance.
- Positive, constructive effects of conflict include the fact that learning occurs, it is motivating, positions can be clarified, divergent views considered, competition encouraged, change and innovation facilitated and pressure released.
- Conflict has the potential to damage the organisation; it should therefore be managed effectively, constructively and productively.

Dysfunctional conflict:

- Conflict is abnormal and unnatural.
- Conflict is harmful and hinders the achievement of goals.
- Conflict is a waste of management time.
- Employee energy is used in inappropriate directions.
- Conflict can be destructive and reduce levels of job satisfaction and performance and increase absenteeism and turnover.

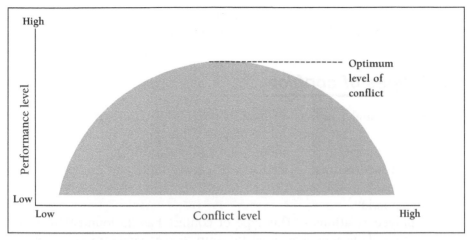

Figure 10.2 Relationship between levels of conflict and organisational performance

10.2 Sources of conflict

Huczynski and Buchanan (1991) identified five common causes of conflict in organisations:

1. **The employment relationship** – The employer and employee often have different objectives. The employer requires productivity, cost-effectiveness and change, while the employee is searching for security, equitable rewards and opportunity. Issues creating conflict include working time, work flow and task allocation.
2. **Resource allocation** – Resources are required for product development, financial investment and the development of human resources. Conflict may exist between people (inter-individual conflict), between groups, teams or departments (inter-group conflict) and within a group, team or department (intra-group conflict).
3. **Role ambiguity** – Conflict may be caused when people are unclear about their role in the organisation and what is expected of them from their supervisor and co-workers. Conflict can be reduced by ensuring that the lines of authority and responsibility are clear.
4. **Interdependence** – When individuals or work groups rely on each other to achieve adequate work flow and quality of work, conflict can arise if standards are not maintained.
5. **Differentiation** – This can be defined as the extent to which the tasks of individuals or groups are divided. Differences between people can lead to the development of distinct work groups, or cliques. These groups can

develop their own norms, values and practices that may create divisions between people. This may lead to an 'in group, out group' situation.

10.3 Types of conflict

- **Interpersonal conflict** – This occurs between two or more individual employees or managers and employees. This type of conflict may result from differences in perception, belief and personality.
- **Inter-group conflict** – This happens between different groups, units or departments over issues such as resource allocation, interdependence and differentiation.
- **Employee relations** – This type of conflict has its foundation in the structure of the employment relationship. Two general forms of employee relations conflict can be identified, individual and collective:
  - Unorganised, *individual conflict,* which is spontaneous, reactive and random, such as absenteeism, turnover, theft or acts of sabotage.
  - Organised, *collective conflict* – Systematic collective efforts resulting in co-ordinated action, such as strikes, go-slows, overtime bans or the withdrawal of co-operation.
- **Inter-organisational conflict** – This may result from a dispute between organisations as they compete for customers, market share or over issues of patents or copyright.

10.4 Perspectives on conflict

Four different perspectives on conflict have been identified to provide an understanding of the various approaches adopted by management to conflict situations. The beliefs held about whether conflict is functional or dysfunctional influence the style of management and the experience employees have in the workplace, and have consequences for the organisation.

Unitarist perspective

Beliefs:

- Harmony and unity are the natural state.
- Conflict is an abnormal phenomenon.
- If conflict exists, something has gone wrong that has to be fixed.
- Failure has occurred in the normal functioning of the organisation.

- Problems may exist due to poor communication, inadequate management or troublemakers.
- Conflict is negative and damaging.
- Conflict upsets the normal harmonious and productive environment.
- Conflict may be handled by eradicating the source and/or avoiding it.

Characteristics of management style:

- Unified team is very important.
- Need to maintain team spirit.
- Everyone works for the good of the organisation.
- Emphasis is on the achievement of organisational goals.
- Management is the source of authority.
- Loyalty and commitment must be given to management.
- Troublemakers do not share the common interests of the organisation or accept authority.
- Agitators endanger organisational success.
- Employees must fall in line or risk elimination.
- Closed style of management.

Organisational consequences:

- Stable environment.
- Rules and regulations defined.
- Clarity of roles and responsibilities.
- Low levels of participation and involvement by employees.
- Reduced job satisfaction and organisational commitment.
- Difficulties embracing change.
- High levels of absenteeism and turnover.
- Low morale.
- Possible occurrence of acts of sabotage.

Pluralist perspective

Beliefs:

- Conflict is a naturally occurring phenomenon.
- Conflict is inherent in organisations as they are made up of a collection of groups.
- Conflict is inevitable; it should be expected, planned for and managed effectively.
- Conflict should be managed rather than eliminated.

Characteristics of management style:

- Recognition that individuals and groups have different objectives.
- Functional conflict should be channelled.
- Dysfunctional conflict must be eliminated.
- Reconciliation of conflicting interests between individuals and groups.
- Compromise and negotiation are utilised.
- Open style of management.

Organisational consequences:

- Higher levels of participation and involvement by employees.
- Increased job satisfaction and organisational commitment.
- Enhanced relationships between management and employees.
- Consideration of employee needs.
- Lower resistance to change.
- Reduced absenteeism and turnover.
- Morale enhanced.

Interactionist perspective

Beliefs:

- Conflict is viewed as a positive and necessary force.
- Conflict is seen as inevitable.
- Conflict leads to effective performance.
- If conflict does not exist, it should be stimulated and a means of resolution sought.
- Harmony and unity dull initiative and innovation.
- An appropriate level of conflict stimulates creativity and innovation.
- Change and new thinking arise from conflict, which can lead to the creation of a new work environment.

Impact on employees and organisational consequences:

- Creation of a dynamic environment.
- Workplace may be viewed as tough or abrasive.
- Level of conflict may produce a degree of turnover.
- Change becomes the norm.
- Organisation rapidly adjusts to changing environment, leading to success.

Radical perspective

- Conflict is an inevitable result of capitalism.
- Based on Marxist theory of capitalist society and social change.

- Belief that an inherent struggle exists between employer (representing capital) and employee (representing labour).
- An unequal distribution of power exists between the dominant establishment group, including employers and shareholders, and the workers.
- This struggle represents a broader class struggle in society.
- Revolutionary change is needed to dismantle the capitalist system and redistribute power in favour of workers and the working class, thereby producing a classless society.

The four perspectives produce a framework for evaluating the strengths and weaknesses of management behaviour in conflict situations.

10.5 Conflict handling and resolution

According to Thomas (1976), conflict can be categorised along two dimensions:

1. **Assertiveness** – This is a person's desire to satisfy only his or her own concerns.
2. **Co-operation** – This is a person's willingness to satisfy the other party's concerns.

Thomas (1976) has developed a framework to present five alternative approaches to handling conflict (see Figure 10.3).

Competition can be used when:

- Goals are incompatible.
- Quick, decisive action is necessary.
- Future popularity of the decision is unimportant.
- The matter is essential to organisational success.
- One or both parties may take advantage.

Avoidance can be used when:

- It is a trivial issue.
- Neither party will satisfy concerns.
- Disruption must be ended.
- People need to cool down.
- More information is needed.
- Hidden agendas exist.

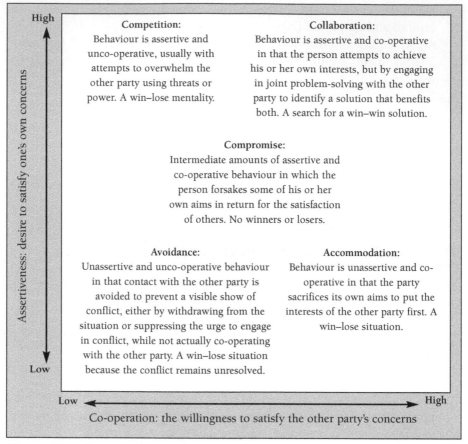

Figure 10.3 Alternative approaches to handling conflict (after Thomas, 1976)

Compromise can be used when:

• Goals are important but not worth disruption.
• Parties have equal power.
• Temporary settlement is needed.
• Time is short.

Accommodation can be used when:

• Goals are incompatible.
• One party is clearly wrong.
• Issue is more vital to one party.
• Trade-off has to be established.
• One party needs to retreat with dignity.
• One side needs to learn from its mistakes.

Collaboration can be used when:

- Interaction is important to goal attainment.
- Goals are compatible
- Time is plentiful.
- Both sides need to learn from the experience.
- Commitment of both sides is agreed.
- Emotions that would cause further conflicts can be worked through.

The style of conflict resolution chosen should be appropriate to the situation. Effective conflict management produces high levels of group performance.

10.6 Conclusion

Conflict results from the perceptions of two or more parties that are operating in opposition to each other. It results in feelings of discomfort and hostility. Conflict has benefits for an organisation, but can also be harmful and hinder progress. A number of factors cause conflict in organisations, which can occur between individuals, groups and organisations. The unitarist, pluralist, interactionist and radical perspectives on conflict provide a framework for understanding a range of management styles and how they impact on the experience of employees and the functioning of the organisation. It is important that managers know when to stimulate and when to resolve conflict. There is no one best way to resolve conflict, it is important to understand a range of methods. A contingency perspective, which considers the complexities of the situation, should be adopted. The most effective method of managing conflict should be identified; this will have regard for employees, organisational factors and the wider environment.

Summary

- Definition of conflict.
- Functional and dysfunctional conflict.
- Sources of conflict in organisations.
- Perspectives on conflict.
- Conflict handling and resolution.

Theory to real life

1. Based on your personal experience, identify situations when conflict was functional and situations when it was dysfunctional.

2. Which of the perspectives on conflict best describes your beliefs about conflict?
3. How would, or does, your belief about conflict influence your management style?
4. What do you think are the strengths and weaknesses of your approach to the management of conflict?
5. What advice would you give a manager in a workplace about the best way to manage conflict?

Exercises

1. **Debate:** In class, divide into three groups for a debate. Groups 1 and 2 should have five to six people and Group 3 will be the remaining class members.
    *   **Group 1** should defend the unitarist philosophy that conflict is an aberration to be avoided at all costs.
    *   **Group 2** should defend the pluralist philosophy that conflict is a perfectly natural phenomenon.
    *   **Group 3** should evaluate the presentations and ask questions of both groups, then evaluate which group presented the best argument to support their approach to conflict.
2. Consider how a manager's perspective/frame of reference (unitarist, pluralist, interactionist, radical) influences their perception of the behaviour of employees.
3. Discuss the view that 'an organisation can have too little or too much conflict'.

Essay questions

1. Propose a definition of conflict.
2. Examine the factors that give rise to conflict in organisations.
3. Investigate the distinction between functional and dysfunctional conflict.
4. Describe the four key perspectives on conflict.
5. Name two examples of unorganised, individual conflict.
6. Name two examples of organised, collective conflict.
7. Evaluate the impact of a manager who adopts a unitarist approach to conflict on employees and on the organisation.
6. Evaluate the influence of a manager who adopts a pluralist approach to conflict on employees and on the organisation.

7. Describe the methods of conflict resolution proposed by Thomas (1976).

Short questions

1. Define organisational conflict.
2. Name three factors that give rise to conflict in organisations, according to Huczynski and Buchanan.
3. Explain what is meant by the term 'functional conflict'.
4. Explain what is meant by the term 'dysfunctional conflict'.
5. Name two examples of unorganised, individual conflict.
6. Name two examples of organised, collective conflict.
7. Identify three beliefs held by a manager who adopts the unitarist perspective on conflict.
8. Outline three characteristics of the management style used by a manager who adopts the unitarist approach to conflict.
9. Name three organisational consequences of adopting the unitarist approach to conflict.
10. Identify three beliefs held by a manager who adopts the pluralist perspective on conflict.
11. Outline three characteristics of the management style used by a manager who adopts the pluralist approach to conflict.
12. Name three organisational consequences of adopting the pluralist approach to conflict.
13. Identify three characteristics of the interactionist perspective on conflict
14. Identify two characteristics of the radical perspective on conflict.
15. *Name* and *describe* the two dimensions of conflict resolution, according to Thomas (1976)?
16. Identify the five styles of behaviour that can be engaged in to resolve conflict, according to Thomas (1976).

11
COMMUNICATION IN ORGANISATIONS

Objectives

This chapter will help you to:

- Define communication.
- Identify the significant impact communication has on performance.
- Describe the process of communication.
- Recognise common problems that occur during the process of communication.
- Describe the characteristics of effective communication.

11.1 Communication defined

The ability to communicate effectively is at the core of good management.

Communication has been defined as **the process by which two or more parties exchange information and share meaning** (O'Reilly and Pondy, 1979).

According to Axley (1996), **communication is a process of sending and receiving messages with attached meanings, with the ultimate meaning in any communication being created by the receiver or perceiver of the message**.

The main purpose of communication in the workplace is to co-ordinate the performance of all the parts of the organisation. Communication is a means of controlling the performance of employees; of providing motivation; of emotional expression; and of sharing information. There are many forms of communication, including face-to-face meetings, phone calls, voice mails, e-mails, text messages, post, reports, memos, blogs, video conferencing and information held on intranet and internet sites. The process of communication is frequently taken for granted, yet its impact on employee satisfaction and employee performance should not be underestimated. Effective organisations communicate effectively.

Ludlow and Panton (1992) highlight the significant influence that communication has on performance in organisations:

- Keeps employees in the picture.
- Increases involvement.

- Enhances motivation and commitment.
- Improves relationships.
- Facilitates change.

Channels of communication in organisations are described as being either formal or informal. *Formal channels* follow the chain of command, as identified by the organisational structure, and transmit information relevant to job-related activities. These channels are authoritative and are usually used to communicate policies, procedures and other official information. They generally take the form of meetings, memos, e-mails and voicemails. *Informal channels* coexist with formal channels of communication, but diverge from the organisation's hierarchy of authority. They consist of personal and social messages. Informal channels allow unofficial information and rumours to circulate among networks of friends and acquaintances. This type of channel is referred to as the *grapevine* and gives people a sense of security, gained from knowing what is going on, and a sense of belonging. It satisfies people's social needs and may happen in person, such as in the so-called 'water cooler moments', but also through e-mails, texts and social networks. Rumours can be very dysfunctional at all levels of an organisation and their degree of accuracy should always be questioned.

11.2 Communication process

Communication is a social process and involves the transfer of information between one person, group or organisation to another person, group or organisation. It involves the process of the passage of information from one party to another. This process is best represented by a simple model of communication between two persons: the *sender* and the *receiver.* The sender is the source, or originator, of the communication and the receiver is the recipient of the communication.

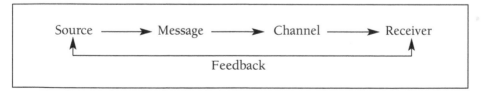

Figure 11.1 The communication process

Source

The source of communication may be an individual, group or organisation. The source is responsible for preparing, encoding and entering the message into the transmission medium.

Encoding

The message is translated by the source from an idea or thought into symbolic form. Symbols include words, numbers, pictures, sounds and gestures. It is important that both the source and receiver attach the same meaning to the symbols in order to avoid ambiguity and confusion. Sources use their skills, attitudes, knowledge and experience to encode the message.

Channel

This is the method of transmitting the message or the vehicle through which the message will flow. The medium that is selected to send a message will have a direct influence on how well that message is transmitted.

Channels of communication include the following:

Method	Advantages	Disadvantages
Telephone	Verbal Interactive Convenient Source receives immediate feedback from receiver	Less personal than face-to-face meetings Possibility of misunderstandings occurring Could be inconveniently timed for receiver
Face to face	Visual, personal contact Rich explanations can be provided Immediate feedback provided	Requires spontaneous thinking Effort required to arrange meeting Power or status may cause pressure
Meetings	Can use visuals Involves several minds Two-way exchange of information	Time-consuming One person may dominate meeting and push their own agenda

Memorandum	Brief
	Provides a record of
	   information
	Can spend time preparing
	   message
	Copies can be distributed
	   widely and at low cost
		No control over the receiver
		Less personal
		One-way flow of information
		Feedback is delayed

Formal report	Complete
	Comprehensive
	Can be disseminated widely
		Less personal
		Considerable time spent in
		   preparation and in reading
		Language may be difficult
		Expensive
		One-way flow of
		   communication
		Delayed feedback

Teleconferencing	Saves time on travel
	Visual
	Reduces impact of power/
	   status
	Parties usually well prepared
		Interpersonal contact lacking
		Not good for initial
		   brainstorming sessions
		Expensive

E-mail	Convenient
	Accessible to most
	Messages can be sent and
	   received 24 hours a day
	Extremely fast
		Can lead to information
		   overload
		Others may be able to get
		   access to messages
		May not always be relevant

Table 11.1 Various channels of communication in organisations

The richness of the communication medium should be the main basis on which decisions are made about how exactly to send a message. Richer media provide multiple cues and rapid feedback.

Decoding

This involves the receiver interpreting the message that has been sent by the source. The receiver is active in this part of the communication process and their understanding is influenced by their skills, attitudes, knowledge and experience. The meaning that the receiver attaches to the symbols may be the same or different to those intended by the source. Breakdowns can occur in the communication process and misunderstandings result.

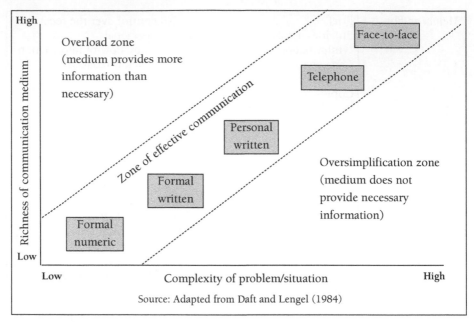

Figure 11.2 Contingency model for selecting communication media

Receiver

This can be an individual, group or organisation. The receiver perceives or interprets the encoded symbols. The receiver may or may not be able to decode the meaning as they try to understand the message sent by the source. It is vital that the receiver is an active and good listener to facilitate the transmission of the message from the source to the receiver.

Feedback

This is an important part of the communication process and involves the receiver returning a message to the sender to acknowledge receipt of the message and to indicate their response. Feedback allows for the verification of the message and therefore ensures that it has been received and understood.

Noise

This refers to any disturbance in the process of communication. Noise can interfere with or distort communication. The type of noise encountered is a function of the medium that is selected. Noise includes poor phone connections, speech impairment, illegible handwriting, poor hearing or eyesight and physical distance.

11.3 Communication problems

Much of the research on the communication process in organisational settings has focused on factors that can increase or decrease its effectiveness. Factors that can affect the flow of communication relate to the source, the processes of encoding and decoding, the receiver, feedback and the organisation itself.

- **Source** – Information may be filtered by the source on the basis that the receiver does not 'need to know'. This may lead the receiver to incorrectly interpret the message or may even render the message meaningless. In order to receive the attention of the receiver, it is important that the source is credible and is trusted.
- **Encoding and decoding** – The encoding skill of the sender is vital to achieve effective communication. This includes the ability to speak and write clearly and to select the appropriate channel for transmitting the information. *Decoding skills* also influence the effectiveness of communication. Research has shown that effective managers have good decoding skills in listening and responding to the needs and concerns of employees. Listening skills are one of the most effective decoding skills that can be used in the workplace.

  In general, difficulties encountered include a lack of common experience in background and culture between the source and receiver. Also, semantics, which involves the study and use of words, may be an issue. Difficulties may be experienced if different meanings areattributed to the same word by the source and the receiver. Finally, jargon, which is technical or specialised language, may be used by the source but may not be understood by the receiver. Jargon serves the purpose of speeding up communication between those who speak the language; it can cause problems when the receiver is not 'fluent' in its use. The use of jargon can also create problems when a team of employees is from different professional disciplines, all of which may use different jargon. In order to achieve clarity in sending a message it may be useful to remember the Kiss principle of communication: **K**eep **i**t **s**hort and **s**imple (Borman, 1982).
- **Channel** – Characteristics of the method of transmission of a message may affect communication. Selection of the appropriate channel can have

an important effect on the accurate flow of communication. The channel selected can also affect the impact of the message and the achievement of the results desired. For example, a face-to-face meeting with a supervisor to recognise high levels of performance will carry more weight than a brief e-mail. When presenting complicated information, the use of multiple channels of communication will increase the likelihood that attention will be paid to the information and it will be retained.

- **Receiver** – In arriving at an understanding of the message that is being communicated, the receiver may place some barriers in the way. The receiver may only pay attention to the part of the message that interests them or they believe applies to them and may disregard the rest. This is referred to as *selective attention*. People also have a tendency to make value judgements about messages they receive. Positive evaluations are made about information that reinforces existing views, while negative evaluations are made about information that challenges an individual's personal beliefs. Value judgements enable people to hear more about what they know and like and less about what is negative and may alter the picture that they have of themselves. There are times when too much information is presented to the receiver and they may become overloaded. The result is selective attention. It is very important that the receiver has the ability to actively listen to the message being sent. It would be of benefit to managers to consider the speak–listen ratio, which highlights the fact that people have one mouth and two ears! Schermerhorn *et al.* (2011) state that active listening means encouraging people to say what they really mean.
- **Feedback** – The benefit of feedback is that it provides clarification, verification and motivation. If feedback is omitted, the process of communication may break down and misinterpretations may result. Managers in organisations are frequently criticised for providing too little feedback.
- **Organisational factors** – Status differences may cause communication problems as, generally, the higher the organisational status of the sender, the more likely the communication will be listened to and acted upon. People are supposed to listen to their bosses! In addition, noise created by organisational politics, gossip, rumours, the use of ineffective channels of information and poorly coded messages can create difficulties. Employees today receive messages through a variety of channels within limited timeframes, leading to information overload.

11.4 Communication flow in organisations

Information flows through communication lines and networks and gives life to the work of organisations. This communication flow is usually classified into three types. It can flow:

* *Downward,* through the organisational hierarchy.
* *Upward,* through the same chain of command.
* *Laterally,* from colleague to colleague.

Downward communication

This follows the chain of command and is made up of messages sent from superiors to subordinates. Most commonly, it consists of:

* Instructions or directions concerning job performance.
* Information about organisational procedures and policies.
* Feedback to subordinates concerning job performance.
* Information to assist in the co-ordination of work tasks.

While much formal communication in organisations is downward, research indicates that employees would like more information from their superiors about work procedures and about what is happening throughout the organisation.

In addition, it appears from studies that certain types of downward communication may be particularly limited, for example, feedback about work performance. This is particularly true in companies that fail to conduct regular performance appraisals. The lack of this type of information impacts directly on the level of job satisfaction experienced by employees.

Upward communication

This is the flow of information from the lower levels of the organisation to the upper levels. It normally consists of information managers need to perform their jobs, such as feedback about the status of lower-level operations, which could include reports of production output or information about any difficulties experienced by employees. The upward flow of information is essential for managers in order to make important work-related decisions. In addition, upward communication can consist of complaints and suggestions for improvement from lower-level workers and is significant because it gives subordinates some involvement in the functioning of the organisation.

Lateral communication

This is the flow of messages between people who are on the same level in an organisation and is especially important when co-workers have to co-ordinate their activities in order to achieve a goal as part of a team or task force. Lateral communication can also occur between cross-departmental committees, for example between the sales, production and quality control departments. Lateral communication facilitates the sharing of news and information and helps develop interpersonal relationships.

11.5 Enhancing communication in organisations

Several strategies can be used to enhance the flow of communication in organisations.

- **Employee suggestion schemes** – Workers can submit ideas in a variety of ways and can be encouraged by some sort of incentive or bonus scheme based on the amount of savings the suggestion produces. This can increase participation and involvement and lead to innovations, but a downside is that the suggestion system may be used to voice complaints about conditions that management are unable to change.
- **Open-door policies** – This involves identifying times when employees can go directly to managers to discuss whatever is on their minds. It provides a direct line of communication to management, communicating the message that employees' views and experiences are important and that consideration will be given to their needs. An obvious problem is the danger of managers using their time on what may be trivial matters.
- **Grievance systems** – These are designed to change existing negative situations and must be handled delicately. The channel of communication must be kept open, initially to acknowledge receipt of the grievance by company officials and during the process to make it clear what action has been taken.
- **Employee attitude surveys** – This is an efficient method to measure employee attitudes in order to target problem areas or to get ideas for improvement. Feedback from management is very important to provide the respondents with the impression that their opinions are valuable.

Characteristics of effective communication

Dawson (1996) identified the central characteristics of effective communication:

- **Accuracy** – The message that is received should clearly reflect intention and truth.
- **Reliability** – The communication should convey the same message/meaning to anyone receiving it.
- **Validity** – The information transmitted should capture reality, be consistent, allow prediction and contain established knowledge.
- **Adequacy** – The right amount of information should be given at the right time.
- **Effectiveness** – The message should achieve the intended result from the sender's point of view.

11.6 Conclusion

Communication in organisations has become more important due to increased collaboration at all levels. It involves the exchange of information and meaning and is said to be the glue that holds an organisation together. The management of communication in organisations involves an understanding of the process and the problems that can arise. An appreciation of these barriers and how they can be overcome will lead to more effective communication. Current issues in communication include the rapid pace of technological developments, workforce diversity, globalisation and the increasing use of social networks. There is no one best way to communicate, but an awareness and consideration of the audience and their needs is required at all times. Organisations are involved in communicating with a wide range of people within the organisation, but also to others outside the organisation such as stakeholders, suppliers and customers. Communication is a tool and the effective use of it by organisations will bring many benefits.

Summary

- Definition of communication.
- Process of communication.
- Communication problems.
- Communication flow in organisations.
- Enhancing communication in organisations.
- Characteristics of effective communication.

Theory to real life

1. In your view, what parts of the communication process are done inadequately or left out when sending a message by text or e-mail?
2. Evaluate the methods of communication that you use frequently.
3. Identify the formal and informal communication networks that exist in your college and/or place of work.
4. Why is good communication important to a successful business?

Exercises

1. In class, discuss the benefits of adopting a contingency model for selecting communication media.
2. Identify the sources of noise that affect the communication process in your lectures and/or your workplace.
3. Suggest a number of strategies that can be used to increase upward communication flow from workers to management.

Essay questions

1. Propose a definition of communication.
2. Examine the stages in the communication process.
3. Investigate the barriers that exist to effective communication.
4. Examine the main differences between downward, upward and lateral communication in organisations.
5. Describe how communication flow can be enhanced in an organisation.
6. Identify the characteristics of effective communication.

Short questions

1. According to O'Reilly and Pondy (1979), communication is the process by which two or more parties exchange _____ and share _____.
2. According to Axley (1996), who creates the ultimate meaning in any communication?
3. What is the difference between a formal and an informal channel of communication?
4. What is meant by the statement 'people cannot not communicate'?
5. Name three benefits of organisational communication.

6. Draw a diagram of the communication process.
7. Describe each of the stages of the communication process.
8. What is the term given to any disturbance in the communication process?
9. Examine the problems relating to each stage of the communication process.
10. Why is it necessary to adopt a contingency model for selecting communication media?
11. Name three types of communication in organisations.
12. What are the five characteristics of effective communication, according to Dawson (1996)?

12
ORGANISATIONAL CHANGE

Objectives

This chapter will help you to:

- Understand the nature of organisational change.
- Describe the triggers for change.
- Understand the reactions that people have to organisational change.
- Identify the organisational sources of resistance to change.
- Describe the individual sources of resistance to change.
- Evaluate methods of managing resistance to change.

12.1 Organisational change defined

Organisations today exist in dynamic and ever-changing environments that demand rapid and significant responses. The success and future survival of an organisation depends on its ability to adapt to the demands made on it from inside and outside the organisation. Demands include the training and development of employees, recruitment and selection of new employees and the enhancement of products and services in line with the demands of the marketplace. According to Ford and Ford (1995), change means that '**an organisation shifts from one state to another**'. The structure and functioning of the organisation should mirror the environment in which it operates and therefore it constantly has to make changes to more effectively meet the needs of customers, employees and shareholders, to incorporate developments in technology and to reflect social and political pressures. Tersine *et al.* (1997) state that:

> change has joined death and taxes as life certainties. Some businesses have been quick to accept and adopt changes; others are struggling to cope with it. Specialists and individualism have been replaced by teams and co-operation. People are being asked to do more with less on a regular basis from a litany of change, innovate, re-engineer, continuously improve, and then change again.

This statement highlights the reality of organisational change as a continuing process that often creates difficulties for people and organisations. Once a change is complete, it is time to initiate another change.

Kurt Lewin (1951), the founding father of planned change, contended that organisational change was a dynamic process rather than a one-off event. He asserted that change involved the need to:

- *Unfreeze*, by making people aware of the need for change and destabilising the current state of affairs or status quo.
- *Move* to a desired new state by abandoning old behaviour and adopting new behaviour.
- *Refreeze*, by establishing the new pattern of behaviour as the normal way to function.

Lewin's model of planned change provided a general framework for understanding the process of organisational change. However, in today's dynamic environment, where ongoing change is the norm, refreezing may not be an option. Buchanan and Huczynski (2010) assert that a state of 'permanent thaw' is a more appropriate description.

Nadler and Tushman (1986) identified different types of organisational change. They described two dimensions along which change can be categorised:

1. Scope of change – incremental or strategic.
2. Timing of change – anticipatory or reactive.

A four-part typology of change was then presented (see Figure 12.1).

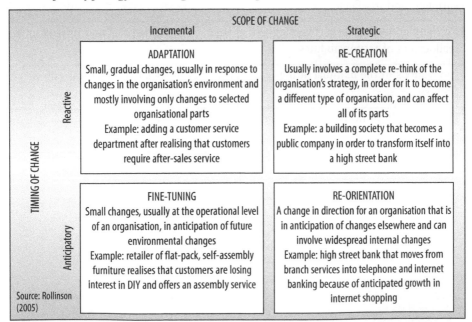

Figure 12.1 A typology of organisational change (after Nadler and Tushman, 1986)

12.2 Triggers for change

The process of organisational change can be caused by many different triggers for change. Buchanan and Huczynski (2010) describe triggers for change as '*disorganizing pressures indicating that current systems, procedures, rules, organization structures and processes are no longer effective*'.

The forces for change can be described as *internal* and *external*. Internal changes refer to those caused by factors inside the organisation and external to those caused by sources outside the organisation.

Internal triggers for change	External triggers for change
New product and service design innovations	Changing economic and trading conditions, domestic and global
Low performance and morale, high stress and staff turnover	New technology and materials
Appointment of a new senior manager or top management team	Changes in customers' requirements and tastes
Inadequate skills and knowledge base, triggering training programmes	Activities and innovations of competitors; mergers and acquisitions
Office and factory relocation, closer to suppliers and markets	Legislation and government policies
Recognition of problems triggering reallocation of responsibilities	Shifts in local, national and international politics
Innovations in the manufacturing process	Changes in social and cultural values
New ideas about how to deliver services to customers	
Source: Buchanan and Huczynski (2010)	

Table 12.1 Internal and external triggers for organisational change

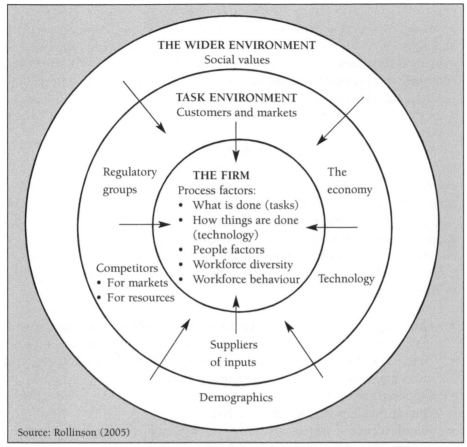

Figure 12.2 Triggers for change in organisations

12.3 Resistance to change

'Resistance to change is an emotional/behavioural response to real or imagined threats to an established work routine' (Kreitner and Knicki, 2001).

'Resistance to change is any attitude or behaviour that indicated unwillingness to make or support a desired change' (Schermerhorn *et al.*, 2011).

Buchanan and Huczynski (2010) see resistance to change as 'an unwillingness, or an inability to accept or to discuss changes that are perceived to be damaging or threatening to the individual'.

Organisational change has many benefits, yet it is frequently resisted at the level of the individual and the organisation. People are cautious about the effects of change and managers need to learn to manage resistance. Resistance arises out of a need in employees to defend that which is important to them and appears to be threatened by the change process. Leaders may try to overcome resistance in order to implement change successfully. However, resistance can provide useful information about how employees perceive the planned change and their reasons for concern. Failed attempts to manage resistance to change can lead to lower levels of employee loyalty and of goal achievement.

Resistance to change is a common phenomenon and may occur on a cognitive, affective or behavioural level. Therefore it may affect how employees think, feel and behave during a time of change. The positive aspect of resistance is that it produces stability and predictability. The negative side of resistance is that it hinders individual and organisational adaptation and progress. Baron and Greenberg (1992) have identified common categories of reactions to change. They describe seven types of behaviours demonstrated by individuals when faced with change in the organisation:

- **Quitting** – Change is perceived to be intolerable by individuals, who believe that they have no choice but to leave the organisation.
- **Active resistance** – Individuals personally defy the change initiative and encourage others to resist its implementation.
- **Opposition** – A lack of co-operation in the change process is demonstrated, which results in delays.
- **Acquiescence** – People feel unhappy with changes but feel powerless and therefore put up with the changes.
- **Reserved acceptance** – Overall change is accepted by individuals, but a number of details may be bargained over.
- **Acceptance** – Passive co-operation is demonstrated by employees with no overt desire to participate in the change process.
- **Active support** – Change is welcomed and the permanence of the initiative is encouraged.

Source: Baron and Greenberg (1992)

Figure 12.3 Range of categories of reactions to change

Research conducted by Worral and Cooper (2006) into the management experience of change revealed that pressure to cut costs, intensify work and enhance performance was having a negative effect on loyalty, morale, job security and employees' sense of well-being. The factors influencing well-being included unmanageable workloads; little control over aspects of the job; poor work–life balance; not having enough time to do the job to the best of their ability; working longer hours than desired; no influence over performance targets; unrealistic objectives; not being involved in decision-making; and their ideas and suggestions not being taken into consideration.

12.4 Sources of resistance

Opposition to change can occur at the level of the organisation and/or the individual or both. Organisational sources of resistance have been identified that describe common barriers to the introduction of change presented by structural and human factors. Individual sources of resistance originate from a person's perception of the situation, their personality characteristics and their needs. These factors influence their level of motivation to embrace or resist change.

Organisational sources of resistance

Katz and Kahn (1978) identified six commonly encountered sources of organisational resistance to change. Due to their structures, systems and beliefs, organisations can put up barriers preventing the implementation of change.

Overdetermination/Structural inertia

Organisations create systems that produce stability. These include:

*   Selection processes
*   Job descriptions
*   Training programmes
*   Performance reviews
*   Reward systems.

These methods of managing the performance of individuals in the workplace ensure that if they are repeatedly carried out in the same manner, the organisation and its people will remain the same and not embrace change and respond effectively to the ever-changing environment. The organisation is then overly determined in its present and future behaviour by how it has acted in the past. The result is that the status quo is maintained and the system is characterised by **overdetermination,** or **structural inertia.**

Narrow focus of change

An organisation is made up of a number of parts or subsystems. The organisation may, for example, be divided by service or product. Although the different departments such as finance, marketing and human resources operate as distinct entities, they are interdependent. A decision that is made about the expansion of the organisation or the development of a new product will have implications for all departments. In order to be successful, all parts of the organisation must be considered, including people, tasks and structure, and must act as a whole. As all the subsystems are interdependent, they rely on each other to produce results that will lead to an efficient and effective organisation.

Often organisations introduce change in one area or subsystem without considering the implications and the need for change in other related areas. An example of this would be if the senior management in a company manufacturing computer hardware decided that to increase market share they would greatly increase the commission paid to the sales team. The sales staff become highly motivated and produce great results. This increase in orders for the company's computers puts pressure on the production department, which has not made any changes to its work system because it has not been informed of the change decision. The result is that due to the narrow focus of change, the sales team are selling computers that the production team will not be able to produce in time.

The big and wide picture of change and its implications needs to be recognised at an organisational level in order to reduce resistance.

Group inertia

Individual employees often regard change with a sense of excitement, anticipation and enhanced motivation. Even though a number of people may want to embrace the change and adapt their behaviour to meet their own needs and the requirements of the organisation, group norms may act as a constraint. Norms can be defined as a regular pattern of thinking or behaving that a group has adopted; if people want to remain in the group, it is important that these norms, or normal ways of acting, are demonstrated. Resistance to change emerges at the level of the group from accepted norms in relation to production targets, timekeeping, level of attendance at work and willingness to accept change. These norms are not questioned and employees work together in a consistent manner to produce stability, but one which hinders the introduction of change.

Threatened expertise

Resistance may occur at the level of the organisation when change threatens the specialised expertise that individuals and groups have developed over the years. This may occur due to a job redesign or a structural change that may transfer responsibility for a specialised task from the current expert to someone else or even to a piece of technology. For example, over the past number of years, organisational change has resulted in the transformation of the printing industry. The expertise that printers have developed over a lifetime has been threatened and replaced in many cases by the introduction of new technology. At the level of the organisation, fears about the consequences of change produce resistance.

Threatened power

The authority to make decisions gives individuals and groups power. If organisational change occurs and causes the redistribution of long-established power relationships, resistance is a common phenomenon. People like having control over what happens to them and others around them; it provides them with status and influence. The structures of many organisations have been examined and subsequent restructuring has taken place to produce leaner, fitter, flatter structures. One of the many consequences is a decentralised decision-making system that results in a loss of power for managers. The power base of middle managers has been negatively affected by such change, while the line manager has benefited considerably. This threat to power may also arise and cause resistance when introducing teamworking in an organisation.

Resource allocation

Groups in organisations that control important resources frequently regard change as a threat and have a tendency to be content with the way things are. Change may be resisted because it may threaten current resources such as budgets and staffing levels. These changes may affect the payment of bonuses, the recruitment of additional seasonal help, the provision of training and the purchase of new equipment. People may fear that they will be expected to do more for less and may therefore resist change.

Individual sources of resistance

The sources of resistance at an individual level originate from basic human characteristics, including how a person subjectively perceives organisational change. People's reactions to change are also influenced by factors such as whether they are an extrovert or an introvert and their level of emotional stability and other characteristics central to their personality. Finally, people are motivated to accept change to the degree that they believe the results will meet their needs now and in the future.

The following individual sources of resistance have been identified by Zaltman and Duncan (1977) and Nadler (1983):

- **Habit** – As an individual undertakes a job in the same way every day, the work becomes increasingly easy. Learning to work in a different way, with new technology and/or with new people, takes time and effort to get used to. When there is no incentive to change, people retain the old habits that help them to complete their job in a manner they believe is effective.

- **Security** – Change threatens people's fundamental need for security. Therefore, they are likely to resist it. Individuals want and need to feel secure about the task they are completing, the people they are working with and the place they are working in. Change may undermine this feeling of safety and may be resisted.

- **Economic factors** – Organisational change may pose a threat to employees' steady income and fear may exist that jobs could become obsolete during the change process. In addition, changes in job tasks and well-established work routines can create fears in people that they may not be able to perform to the expected standards. This is of particular concern when there is a close relationship between pay and productivity, for example, performance-related pay systems.

- **Fear of the unknown** – It is normal for people to be afraid of something that is not familiar to them. At work, employees become familiar with their colleagues, their supervisors, their job and the environment. This level of familiarity facilitates the effective completion of tasks. Change may cause people to experience anxiety and fear because they do not know what the future may hold and what impact change will have on them.

- **Lack of awareness** – People have a highly subjective view of the world. Perceptual limitations, including lack of attention and/or selective attention, can result in an individual not being aware of a change in the workplace. Due to the fact that they do not recognise that a change has occurred in a rule or procedure, they may not change their behaviour. A lot of the time, individuals only pay attention to information that reinforces their view of the world and disregard other information. Therefore, due to a lack of awareness, they continue to engage in their usual practices.

- **Social factors** – As we are social animals, being part of the group is very important to us. Frequently, employees resist change because they are afraid of what other people will think of them. Individuals may feel that change will affect their image when, for example, they volunteer to become involved in a training programme, accept a promotion or transfer to another department. People fear being perceived as being different to others or ultimately being rejected from the group. The group is a powerful motivator of behaviour and causes resistance to change.

12.5 Managing resistance

Change is vital to the success of every organisation. Resistance produces stability and hinders adaptation and therefore needs to be managed effectively. Resistance can be constructive and it can open up communication between employees and managers; it can cause a re-evaluation of the change decision; and can result in examining new ways to achieve the desired results. This process may produce outcomes which are different to the way the change was originally presented.

Managers should perceive resistance as having benefits and as creating opportunities to enhance the change process. As resistance is grounded in fears and subjective evaluations, management needs to provide employees with information, involve them in the change process and ultimately motivate them to accept change. Managers need to decrease resistance and increase acceptance of change.

Kotter and Schlesinger (1979) identified six methods for dealing with resistance to change:

1. **Education and communication** – Employees should be provided with information about the change process prior to its implementation. The reasons for the change should be fully explained and the communication process should be two-way. This helps to overcome resistance that is grounded in inaccurate and inadequate information and fears of the unknown. The presentation of all the facts can help clear up misunderstandings and reduce resistance. This approach creates support for the change, but can be time-consuming.
2. **Participation and involvement** – This may involve employees being asked for their ideas or advice and/or the appointment of task forces or committees. Bringing those involved into the decision process before a change occurs provides them with a sense of ownership. It is difficult for people to resist a change decision in which they have been involved. The adoption of this strategy is particularly beneficial when employee commitment is essential to successful implementation. The participation and involvement of the employees can be time-consuming and must be managed properly, but it provides a great sense of power and control.

3. **Facilitation and support** – Management may need to provide extra training and support until employees become accustomed to the new system of work. By providing people with knowledge and skills and recognition and encouragement, fears about security and fears of the unknown can be combated. This method of managing resistance takes time and effort and should be managed strategically.

4. **Negotiation and agreement** – The decision by management to enter into negotiation with employees usually occurs when people are losing something significant in the change process and have enough power to resist. Employees may fear the loss of their jobs, reduction in pay or changes in reporting relationships or work groups. Management may be keen to reach agreement with employees because they may form a large group, they may have specialised knowledge or skills or widespread public support, all of which gives them power. Negotiations should take place before change is implemented. This assists in the smooth introduction of change and, if problems arise, both parties can refer back to the negotiated agreement.

5. **Manipulation and co-optation** – Managers may use methods such as manipulating information, resources and favours in order to overcome resistance.

   • *Manipulation* involves a hidden or covert attempt to influence employees by twisting and distorting facts, withholding undesirable information and creating false rumour as a method of reducing resistance.

   • *Co-optation* involves both manipulation and participation. Leaders of a resistance group are 'bought off' or brought on side through flattery and by providing them with what is perceived to be a central role in the decision-making process. Management ask representatives of groups which are likely to be resistant to become involved in the design and implementation of change. The manager may or may not be really interested in their views, but it is a way of reducing resistance and increasing acceptance.

   These methods are quite easy and cost-effective ways to lower resistance, but they can have negative consequences if the people concerned become aware that they are being tricked or used.

6. **Coercion** – This approach involves the use of direct threats or force to lower resistance, and may be adopted when the change agent has power and when speed is important. Employees may be coerced into going along with the change decision by the use of threats of job losses, pay reductions, transfers to different departments or locations or negative performance evaluations. This method may be used due to poor management or when all other attempts have failed. Coercion can have

serious negative effects on the attitudes of employees and produce serious long-term consequences such as sabotage, increased staff turnover and the company gaining a poor reputation.

The process of organisational change is a continuing reality for organisations. Management must have a clear understanding of the need for change, the causes of resistance to change and the methods available to manage resistance effectively. When the process of change is completed, it starts all over again!

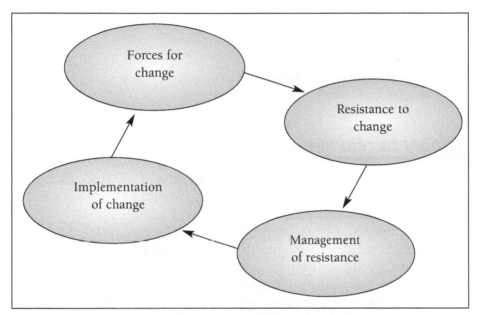

Figure 12.4 Cyclical nature of organisational change

12.6 Conclusion

John C. Maxwell (1998) states that 'change is inevitable. Growth is optional.' It is of key importance in the dynamic and challenging environments in which organisations operate that they grasp the need for ongoing change and development. Change is triggered by many forces internal and external to the organisation. Change management can be viewed by employees as an opportunity or a threat, and their view will influence how they respond to the process of change. Sources of resistance originate at the level of the organisation and the individual. Managers are primary change agents in organisations and should be aware that the decisions they make and the behaviours they display shape the organisation's change culture. There are a range of methods available to managers for dealing with resistance to change.

The approach adopted to the management of change should always consider the needs of the individual employees and teams, the organisation and the operating environment. There is no one best way to manage change, a contingency approach needs to be adopted.

Summary

- Nature of organisational change.
- Triggers for change.
- Resistance to change defined.
- Organisational sources of resistance.
- Individual sources of resistance.
- Managing resistance.

Theory to real life

1. Identify the changes that have happened in your life (such as leaving school, starting college, accepting a new job) and consider your reaction and experience of resistance to change.
2. In your opinion, why do people resist change?
3. What changes are occurring in organisations today?
4. Describe the impact that organisational change has on employees.
5. Name two organisations that have successfully adapted to change.
6. What advice would you give to a manager who is about to introduce change in a workplace?

Exercises

1. In class, divide into groups of four. Each group should identify a successful organisation and the factors it believes have led to this success. Then each group should think of an organisation that it believes is struggling to accept change and is not as efficient and effective as it could be and discuss the changes that the organisation needs to make to enhance its performance. Each group nominates a spokesperson and briefly presents the group's views to the class.
2. In class or tutorial group, consider the benefits and costs of managing resistance to change using the methods proposed by Kotter and Schlesinger (1979). There could be six groups for this task, each evaluating a different method of managing resistance and communicating its findings to the class, perhaps using a role play.

3. Research an organisation currently undergoing change and write a report detailing the nature of the change; the reasons why the change has occurred; the reactions of employees; and how the change is reported to have been managed.
4. Read *Who Moved My Cheese?* the best-selling book about organisational change (Johnson, 2002). What is your cheese? Which character are you most like in your approach to change?

Essay questions

1. Describe the nature and importance of organisational change.
2. Investigate the triggers for organisational change.
3. Describe the four types of change identified by Nadler and Tushman (1986).
4. Provide an explanation of the term 'resistance to change'.
5. Examine the organisational sources of resistance to change.
6. Describe the individual sources of resistance to change.
7. Outline and evaluate the methods identified by Kotter and Schlesinger (1979) for dealing with resistance to organisational change.

Short questions

1. According to Ford and Ford (1995), change means an organisation shifting from _____.
2. Identify the stages in Lewin's model of planned change.
3. Identify two internal triggers that result in organisational change.
4. Name two external forces for change in organisations.
5. Name one positive and one negative aspect of resistance to organisational change.
6. Describe the meaning of the term 'overdetermination'.
7. Name two other sources of organisational resistance to change.
8. Name two individual sources of resistance to organisational change.
9. What are the benefits of using the methods of participation and involvement to manage resistance to organisational change?
10. When and with whom should negotiations be entered into as a method of managing resistance to organisational change?
11. What does coercion involve in terms of the implementation of organisational change?
12. There is no one best way to effectively manage resistance to change; therefore a contingency approach should be adopted. TRUE/FALSE?

REFERENCES

Adams, J.S. (1963) 'Toward an Understanding of Inequity'. *Journal of Abnormal and Social Psychology*, November, pp. 422–436.

Alderfer, C.P. (1972) *Existence, Relatedness, and Growth*. New York: Free Press.

Allinson, S. (1990) 'Personality and Bureaucracy' in R. Wilson and S. Rosenfeld (eds.) *Managing Organizations: Experiences, Texts and Cases*. New York: McGraw-Hill.

Arnold, J. and Randall, R. (2010) *Work Psychology: Understanding Human Behaviour in the Workplace*. 5th ed. Harlow and New York: Financial Times Prentice-Hall.

Arnold, J., Cooper, C.L. and Robertson, I.T. (2005) *Work Psychology: Understanding Human Behaviour in the Workplace*. 4th ed. London: Financial Times Prentice-Hall.

Arroba, T. and James, K. (1991) *Pressure at Work: A Survival Guide for Managers*. 2nd ed. Maidenhead: McGraw-Hill.

Atkinson, R.C. and Sheffrin, R.M. (1968) 'Human Memory: A Proposed System and Its Control Processes' in K.W. Spence and J.T. Spence (eds.) *The Psychology of Learning and Motivation. Volume 2*. New York: Academic Press.

Atkinson, R.L., Atkinson, R.C., Smith, E.E. and Bem, D.J. (1993) *Introduction to Psychology*. 11th ed. New York: Harcourt Brace.

Axley, S. (1996) *Communication at Work: Management and the Communication-Intensive Organization*. Westport: Quorum Books.

Bandura, A. (1977) *Social Learning Theory*. Englewood Cliffs, NJ: Prentice-Hall.

Baron, R. and Greenberg, J. (1992) *Behaviour in Organisations*. Boston, MA: Allyn & Bacon.

Barrick, M.R. and Mount, M.K. (1993) 'Autonomy as a Moderator of the Relationships between the Big Five Personality Dimensions and Job Performance'. *Journal of Applied Psychology*, vol. 78, pp. 111–118.

Barrow, M.J. and Loughlin, H.M. (1992) 'Towards a Learning Organization'. *Journal of Industrial and Commercial Training*, vol. 24, no. 1.

Belbin, M. (1993) *Team Roles at Work*. London: Butterworth Heinemann.

Belbin, R.M. (1996) *The Coming Shape of Organization*. London: Butterworth Heinemann.

Bennis, W. (1989) 'Managing the Dream: Leadership in the 21st Century', *Journal of Orgnisational Change Management*, II/1,7.

Bennis, W. and Nanus, B. (1985) *Leaders: The Strategies for Taking Charge*. New York: Harper and Row.

Bernstein, D.A., Clarke-Stewart, A., Penner, L., Roy, E. and Wickens, C. (2000) *Psychology*. 5th ed. New York: Houghton Mifflin.

Bird, C.P. and Fisher, T.D. (1986) 'Thirty Years Later: Attitudes Toward the Employment of Older Workers'. *Journal of Applied Psychology,* vol. 71, no. 3, pp. 515–517.

Blake, R.R. and McCanse, Anne Adams (1991) *Leadership Dilemmas – Grid Solutions.* Houston: Gulf Publishing.

Blake, R.R. and Mouton, J.S. (1964) *The Managerial Grid.* Houston: Gulf Publishing.

Bloisi, W., Cook, C.W. and Huntsaker, P.L. (2003) *Management and Organisational Behaviour.* London: McGraw-Hill.

Borman, E. (1982) *Interpersonal Communication in the Modern Organisation.* 2nd ed. Englewood Cliffs, NJ: Prentice-Hall.

Bratton, J., Sawchuk, P., Forshaw, C., Callinan, M. and Corbett, M. (2010) *Work & Organizational Behaviour.* 2nd ed. Basingstoke: Palgrave Macmillan.

Buchanan, D.A. and Huczynski, A.A. (2010) *Organizational Behaviour.* 7th ed. Harlow and New York: Financial Times Prentice-Hall.

Butler, M. and Rose, E. (eds.) (2011) *Introduction to Organisational Behaviour.* London: Chartered Institute of Personnel and Development.

Caplan, R.D., Cobb, S., French, Jr., J.R.P., Van Harrison, R. and Pinneau, Jr., S.R. (1975) *Job Demands and Worker Health.* HEW Publication No. [NIOSH] 75–160. Washington, DC: US Department of Health, Education and Welfare, pp. 253–254.

Catlette, B. and Hadden, R. (2001) *Contented Cows Give Better Milk: The Plain Truth about Employee Relations and Your Bottom Line.* Jacksonville, FL: Contented Cow Partners.

Costa, P.T. and McCrae, R.R. (1992) *Manual for the Revised NEO Personality Inventory.* Odessa, FL: Psychological Assessment Resources.

Daft, R.L. and Lengel, R.H. (1984) 'Information Richness: A New Approach to Managerial Behavior and Organization Design' in B.M. Staw and L.L. Cummings (eds.) *Research in Organizational Behavior.* Greenwich, CT: JAI Press, p. 199.

Dalal, R.S. (2005) 'A Meta-Analysis of the Relationship among Organizational Citizenship Behaviour and Counterproductive Work Behaviour'. *Journal of Applied Psychology,* vol. 90, pp. 1241–1255.

Dawson, S. (1996) *Analysing Organisations.* London: Macmillan.

Deal, T.E. and Kennedy, A.A. (1982) *Corporate Cultures: The Rites and Rituals of Corporate Life.* Harmondsworth: Penguin Books.

Ellis, S. and Dick, P. (2005) *Introduction to Organizational Behavior.* 3rd ed. London: McGraw-Hill.

Eysenck, H.J. and Wilson, G. (1975) *Know Your Own Personality.* Harmondsworth: Penguin Books.

Festinger, L. (1950) 'Informal Social Communication'. *Psychological Review,* 57, pp. 271–282.

Festinger, L. (1957) *A Theory of Cognitive Dissonance.* Palo Alto, CA: Stanford University Press.

Fiedler, F.E. (1967) *A Theory of Leadership Effectiveness.* New York: McGraw-Hill.

Fiedler, F.E. (1978) 'Situational Control and a Dynamic Theory of Leadership' in B. King, S. Strenfert and F.E. Fiedler (eds.) *Managerial Control and Organizational Democracy.* New York: John Wiley & Sons, p. 114.

Fiedler, F.E. and Chemers, M.M. (1974) *Leadership and Effective Management.* Glenview, IL: Scott, Foresman and Co.

Fleishman, E.A., Harris, E.F. and Burtt, H.E. (1955) *Leadership and Supervision in Industry.* Columbus, OH: Bureau of Educational Research, Ohio State University.

Fletcher, B. (1988) 'The Epidemiology of Occupational Stress' in C.L. Cooper and R. Payne (eds.) *Causes, Coping and Consequences of Stress at Work.* Chichester: Wiley, pp. 3–52.

Ford, J.D. and Ford, L.W. (1995) 'The Role of Conversation in Producing Intentional Change in Organisations'. *Academy of Management Review,* vol. 20, no. 2 pp. 541–570.

Fox, M.L., Dwyer, D.J. and Ganster, D.C. (1993) 'Effects of Stressful Job Demands and Control on Physiological and Attitudinal Outcomes in a Hospital Setting'. *Academy of Management Journal,* vol. 31, no. 2, pp. 289–318.

Freudenberger, H. (1974) *Burnout: The High Cost of High Achievement.* New York: Anchor Press.

Friedman, M. and Rosenman, R.H. (1959a) *Type A Behavior and Your Heart.* New York: Knopf.

Friedman, M. and Rosenman, R. (1959b) 'Association of Specific Overt Behaviour Pattern with Blood and Cardiovascular Findings'. *Journal of the American Medical Association,* vol. 169, pp. 1286–1296.

George, J.M. (1992) 'Extrinsic and Intrinsic Origins of Perceived Social Loafing in Organisations'. *Academy of Management Journal,* vol. 35, no. 1, pp. 191–202.

Gibb, C. (1947) 'The Principles and Traits of Leadership'. *Journal of Abnormal and Social Psychology,* XLII, pp. 267–284.

Gist, M.E. and Mitchell, T.R. (1992) 'Self-efficacy: A Theoretical Analysis of Its Determinism and Malleability'. *Academy of Management Review,* vol. 17, no.2, pp. 183–211.

Goleman, D. (1995) *Emotional Intelligence: Why It Can Matter More than IQ.* New York: Bantam Books.

Goleman, D. (2000) 'Leadership that Gets Results'. *Harvard Business Review,* March/April, pp. 78–90.

Graziano, W.G., Habashi, M.M., Sheese, B.E. and Tobin, R.M. (2007) 'Agreeableness, Empathy, and Helping: A Person X Situation Perspective'. *Journal of Personality and Social Psychology*, October, vol. 93, no.4, pp. 583–599.

Greenberg, J. and Baron, R.A. (2005) *Behavior in Organizations: Understanding and Managing the Human Side of Work*. 9th ed. NJ: Pearson Education.

Griffin, R.W. and Bateman, T.S. (1986) 'Job Satisfaction and Organizational Commitment'. *International Review of Industrial and Organizational Psychology*, pp. 157–188.

Griffin, R.W. and Moorhead, G. (2007) *Organizational Behavior: Managing People and Organizations*. 8th ed. Boston: Houghton Mifflin Company.

Gross, R.D. (1992) *Psychology: The Science of Mind and Behaviour*. London: Hodder and Stoughton.

Herzberg, F., Mausner, B. and Synderman, B. (1959) *The Motivation to Work*. New York: John Wiley and Sons.

Hilton, J.L. and Von Hippel, W. (1996) 'Stereotypes'. *Annual Review of Psychology*, vol. 47, pp. 237–271.

Hodgetts, R.M. (1991) *Organizational Behavior: Theory and Practice*. New York: Macmillan Publishing Company.

Hogan, K. and Stubbs, R. (2003) *Can't Get Through: 8 Barriers to Communication*. Gretna, LA: Pelican Publishing.

Holmes, T.H. and Rahe, R.H. (1967) 'The Social Readjustment Rating Scale'. *Journal of Psychosomatic Research,* vol. 11, pp. 213–218.

House, R. (1971) 'A Path-Goal Theory of Leader Effectiveness'. *Administrative Science Quarterly*, XVI, September, pp. 321–339.

Huczynski, A.A. and Buchanan, D.A. (1991) *Organizational Behaviour: An Introductory Text*. London: Prentice-Hall.

Huczynski, A.A. and Buchanan, D.A. (2001) *Organizational Behaviour: An Introductory Text*. 4th ed. London: Prentice-Hall.

Huczynski, A. and Buchanan, D.A. (2007) *Organizational Behaviour: An Introductory Text*. 6th ed. London: Prentice-Hall.

Ivancevich, J.M., Matteson, M.T., Freedman, S.M. and Philips, J.S. (1990) 'Worksite Stress Management Interventions'. *American Psychologist*, vol. 45, no. 2, pp. 252–261.

Jackson, H. (1988) 'Type-A Managers Stuck in the Middle'. *Wall Street Journal,* 17 June.

Jago, A.G. (1982) 'Leadership: Perspectives in Theory and Research'. *Management Science,* March, pp. 315–336.

James, W. (1890) *The Principles of Pyschology*. New York: Henry Holt.

Janis, I.L. (1972) *Victims of Groupthink*. New York: Houghton Mifflin.

Johnson, S. (2002) *Who Moved My Cheese?* London: Vermillion.

Judge, T.A., Bono, J.E., Ilies, R. and Gerhardt, M.W. (2002) 'Personality and Leadership: A Qualitative and Quantitative Review'. *Journal of Applied Psychology*, vol. 87, no. 4, pp. 765–780.

Kagan, J. and Havemann, E. (1976) *Psychology: An Introduction*. New York: Harcourt Brace Jovanovich, Inc.

Kahn, R.L., Wolfe, D.M., Quinn, R.P., Snoek, J.D. and Rosenthal, R.A. (1964) *Organisational Stress*. New York: Wiley.

Katz, D. (1960) 'The Functional Approach to the Study of Attitudes'. *Public Opinion Quarterly*, vol. 24, pp. 163–204.

Katz, D. and Kahn, R.L. (1978) *The Social Psychology of Organizations*. 2nd ed. New York: John Wiley and Sons.

Kelley, H.H. (1967) 'Attribution Theory in Social Psychology' in D. Levine (ed.) *Nebraska Symposium on Motivation*. Lincoln, NE: University of Nebraska Press.

Kelly, M. (1997) 'Get a Grip on Stress'. *HR Magazine*, February, pp. 51–57.

Kotter, J. and Schlesinger, L. (1979) 'Choosing Strategies for Change'. *Harvard Business Review*, March/April, pp. 106–114.

Kreitner, R. and Kinicki, A. (2001) *Organizational Behaviour*. 5th ed. Boston: McGraw-Hill Higher Education.

Kreitner, R., Kinicki, A. and Buelens, M. (1999) *Organizational Behaviour: First European Edition*. London: McGraw-Hill Publishing Company.

Lazarus, R.S. and Folkman, S. (1984) *Stress, Appraisal and Coping*. New York: Springer.

Lee, C., Ashford, J. and Bobko, P. (1990) 'Ineffective Effects of Type A Behavior and Perceived Control of Worker Performance, Job Satisfaction, and Somatic Complaints'. *Academy of Management Journal*, vol. 33, December, pp. 870–882.

Leman, K. (2001) *The Birth Order Connection*. New York: Revell Publishing.

Lewin, K. (1951) *Field Theory in Social Science*. New York: Harper and Row.

Likert, R. (1961) *New Patterns of Management*. New York: McGraw-Hill.

Locke, E.A. (1976) 'The Nature and Causes of Job Satisfaction' in M.D. Dunette (ed.) *Handbook of Industrial and Organizational Psychology*. Chicago: Rand McNally, pp. 1297–1350.

Ludlow, R. and Panton, F. (1992) *The Essence of Effective Communication*. Hemel Hempstead: Prentice-Hall.

Luthans, F. (2004) *Organizational Behavior*. 10th ed. Boston: McGraw-Hill.

Markin, R.J. (1974) *Consumer Behaviour*. New York: Macmillan.

Maslow, A.H. (1943) 'A Theory of Human Motivation'. *Psychological Review*, vol. 50, July, pp. 370–396.

Maxwell, J.C. (1998) *The 21 Irrefutable Laws of Leadership*. Nashville: Thomas Nelson.

McClelland, D.C. (1961) *The Achieving Society*. New York: Free Press.

McDonagh, J., Linehan, C. and Weldridge, R. (2002) *Behavioural Science for Marketing and Business Students*. 2nd ed. Dublin: Gill & MacMillan.

McGregor, D. (1960) *The Human Side of Enterprise*. New York: McGraw-Hill.

McKenna, E. (1998) *Business Psychology and Organisational Behaviour: A Students' Handbook*. 2nd ed. East Sussex: Psychology Press.

Meehl, P.E. (1956) 'Wanted: A Good Cookbook'. *American Psychologist*, vol. 11, pp. 263–272.

Meyer, J.P. and Allen, N.J. (1991) 'A Three-component Conceptualisation of Organisational Commitment'. *Human Resource Management Review*, vol. 1, pp. 64–98.

Meyer, J.P. and Herscovitch, L. (2001) 'Commitment in the Workplace: Toward a General Model'. *Human Resource Management Review*, vol. 11, no. 3, pp. 299–326.

Miller, G.A. (1956) 'The Magical Number Seven, Plus or Minus Two: Some Limits on Our Capacity for Processing Information'. *Psychological Review*, vol. 63, pp. 81–97.

Mitchell, T.R. (1982) 'Motivation: New Directions for Theory, Research, and Practice'. *The Academy of Management Review*, vol. 7, no. 1, January, pp. 80–88.

Moorhead, G. and Griffin, R.W. (2012) *Managing Organizational Behavior*. 10th ed. Andover: South-Western Cengage Learning.

Morley, M., Moore, S., Heraty, N., Linehan, M. and MacCurtain, S. (2004) *Principles of Organisational Behaviour: An Irish Text*. 2nd ed. Dublin: Gill & Macmillan.

Mowday, R.T., Porter, L.W. and Steers, R.M. (1982) *Employee-organisational Linkages: The Psychology of Commitment, Absenteeism, and Turnover*. New York: Academic Press.

Mullins, L. (1991) *Management and Organisational Behaviour*. London: Pitman.

Mullins, L.J. (2007) *Management and Organisational Behaviour*. 8th ed. Harlow: Pearson Education.

Nadler, D.A. (1983) 'Concepts for the Management of Organizational Change' in J.R. Hackman, E.E. Lawler III and L.W. Porter (eds.) *Perspectives on Behavior in Organizations*. 2nd ed. New York: McGraw-Hill. pp. 551–561.

Nadler, D.A. and Tushman, M. (1986) *Managing Strategic Organisational Change: Frame Binding and Frame Breaking*. New York: Delta Consulting Group.

O'Reilly, C. and Pondy, L.R. (1979) 'Organisational Communication' in G. Moorhead and R. Griffin (1989) *Organizational Behavior*. 3rd ed. Boston: Houghton Mifflin.

Organ, D.W. (1988) *Organizational Citizenship Behavior: The Good Soldier Syndrome*. Lexington, MA: Lexington Books.

Porter, L.W. and Lawler, E.E. (1968) *Managerial Attitudes and Performance.* Homewood, IL: Dorsey Press.

Pugh, D.S. (ed.) (1997) *Organization Theory: Selected Readings.* 4th ed. Harmondsworth: Penguin.

Robbins, S.P. (2005) *Organizational Behavior.* 11th international ed. Upper Saddle River, NJ: Pearson.

Robbins, S.P., Judge, T.A. and Campbell, T.T. (2010) *Organizational Behaviour.* Harlow: Financial Times Prentice-Hall.

Rogers, C.R. (1961) *On Becoming a Person: A Therapist's View of Psychotherapy.* Boston: Houghton Mifflin.

Rollinson, D. (2005) *Organisational Behaviour and Analysis: An Integrated Approach.* 3rd ed. Harlow: Pearson Education.

Schein, E.H. (1988) *Organizational Psychology.* 3rd ed. New York: Prentice-Hall.

Schermerhorn, J.R., Hunt, J.G. and Osborn, R.N. (1985) *Managing Organizational Behavior.* New York: Wiley.

Schermerhorn, J.R., Hunt, J.G. and Osborn, R.N. (1996) *Managing Organizational Behavior.* New York: Wiley.

Schermerhorn, J.R., Hunt, J.G. and Osborn, R.N. (2005) *Organizational Behavior.* 9th ed. New York: Wiley.

Schermerhorn, J.R., Hunt, J.G., Osborn, R.N. and Uhl-Bien, M. (2011) *Organizational Behavior.* 11th ed. New York: John Wiley & Sons.

Selye, H. (1946) 'The General Adaptation Syndrome and the Diseases of Adaptation'. *Journal of Clinical Endocrynology*, vol. 6, pp. 117–231.

Selye, H. (1956) *The Stress of Life.* New York: McGraw-Hill.

Shaw, M.E. (1991) *Group Dynamics: The Psychology of Small Group Behavior.* 3rd ed. New York: McGraw-Hill.

Smith, G.P. (1994) 'Motivation' in W.R. Tracey (ed.) *Human Resources Management and Development Handbook.* 2nd ed. New York: Amacom Books.

Steers, R.M. (1994) *Introduction to Organizational Behavior.* 2nd ed. New York: HarperCollins Publishers.

Steers, R.M. and Porter, L.W. (1991) *Motivation and Work Behavior.* New York: McGraw-Hill.

Stogdill, R. (1948) 'Personal Factors Associated with Leadership: A Survey of the Literature'. *Journal of Psychology,* XXV, pp. 35–71.

Stoner, J. and Freeman, R. (1992) *The Human Side of Enterprise.* New York: McGraw-Hill.

Szilagyi Jr, D. and Wallace Jr, M.J. (1990) *Organizational Behavior and Performance.* 5th ed. Glenview, IL: Scott, Foresman/Little, Brown.

Tersine, T., Harvey, M. and Buckley, M. (1997) 'Shifting Organizational Paradigms: Transitional Management'. *European Management Journal,* XV/1, pp. 45–57.

Thomas, K. (1976) 'Conflict and Conflict Management' in M.D. Dunnette (ed.) *Handbook of Industrial and Organizational Psychology.* Chicago: Rand McNally.

Tobin, R.M., Graziano, W.G., Vanman, E.J. and Tassinary, L.G. (2000) 'Personality, Emotional Experience, and Efforts to Control Emotions'. *Journal of Personality and Social Psychology,* vol. 79, pp. 656–669.

Tuckman, B.W. (1965) 'Development Sequence in Small Groups'. *Psychological Bulletin,* LXIII, pp. 384–399, 419–427.

Tuckman B.W. and Jensen, M.A.C. (1977) 'Stages of Small Group Development Revisited'. *Group and Organizational Studies,* vol. 2, pp. 419–427.

Vroom, V. (1964) *Work and Motivation.* New York: John Wiley and Sons.

Wagner III, J.A. and Hollenbeck, J.R. (2010) *Organizational Behavior: Securing Competitive Advantage.* New York: Routledge.

West, M.A. and Markiewicz, L. (2004) *Building Team-Based Working. A Practical Guide to Organisational Transformation.* Oxford: Blackwell/British Psychological Society.

Whitsett, D.A. and Winslow, E.K. (1967) 'An Analysis of Studies Critical of the Motivation-Hygiene Theory'. *Personnel Psychology,* winter, pp. 391–415.

Williams, K.C. (1981) *Behavioural Aspects of Marketing.* London: Butterworth Heinemann.

Worral, L. and Cooper, C. (2006) 'Short changed'. *People Management,* vol. 12, no. 13, pp. 36–38.

Zaltman, G. and Duncan, R. (1977) *Strategies for Planned Change.* New York: John Wiley & Sons.

GLOSSARY

Agreeableness is a factor influencing human personality and is characterised by a tendency to be pleasant and accommodating in social situations and to get along with others.

Ascribed attributes are beliefs held about the types of attributes that are associated with those who have a particular status or occupation.

Attitudes are a person's evaluations of objects, events and people and are relatively long lasting.

Attribution theory focuses on the ways in which people explain (or attribute) the causes of their own or others' behaviour by linking it to some internal or external factor.

Authoritarianism is a personality-related characteristic that refers to a person's sensitivity to status, formal authority and official rules.

Barnum effect is when people give a high accuracy rating to descriptions of their personality that are supposedly written specifically for them, but are in reality vague and broad enough to apply to a wide range of people.

Behaviourism examines the observable behaviour of people and animals, but not their unobservable mental processes. The behaviourist school of thought asserts that behaviours can be described scientifically without reference to internal physiological events or to thoughts and beliefs.

Burnout occurs when an individual simultaneously experiences increased pressure and decreased sources of satisfaction. It is more likely to be experienced by those who have high aspirations and strong motivation and produces a general feeling of exhaustion.

Channel of communication is a method of transmitting a message. The medium selected will directly influence the effectiveness of the transmission of the message.

Classical/Pavlovian conditioning proposes that learning occurs when a new stimulus begins to elicit behaviour similar to that originally produced by an old stimulus.

Coercion involves the use of direct threats of force to lower employee resistance to change.

Cognitive dissonance is a state of inconsistency between an individual's attitudes and behaviour.

Cognitive structures are patterns of physical or mental action that underlie particular acts of intelligence.

Cohesiveness is the extent to which a group is committed to staying together.

Communication involves two or more parties sending and receiving messages in order to share information and meaning.

Conflict is a social process that begins when a person, group or organisation perceives that another party has frustrated, or is a about to frustrate, the fulfilment of a need. Functional conflict benefits the organisation, whereas dysfunctional conflict damages the organisation.

Conscientiousness is a factor influencing human personality and is characterised by a high level of competence, order, duty, achievement orientation and self-discipline.

Contingency approach, also referred to as the **situational approach**, states that there is no one universally applicable set of management principles or rules to govern organisations. Differences between organisations and situations demand different management approaches.

Control of performance in organisations involves setting performance standards; measuring performance; comparing standard and actual performance; and taking the required corrective action.

Counterproductive work behaviour (CWB) goes against the goals of an organisation and is often related to feelings of job dissatisfaction. It involves the employee purposely disrupting relationships, organisational culture or performance in the workplace.

Differentiation is the extent to which the tasks of individuals are divided. Differences between people can lead to the development of distinct work groups or cliques.

Disposition relates to a person's mood, temperament, state of readiness or tendency to behave in a particular way.

Distress is an unpleasant stress that accompanies negative events.

Diversity in the workplace involves an understanding that each individual is different and unique. Differences exist among people in terms of their age, gender, race, ethnicity, sexual orientation, socio-economic status, physical abilities, religious and political beliefs and other ideologies. The concept of diversity embodies respect and acceptance.

Effectiveness involves accomplishing the expected or intended result.

Efficiency describes the degree to which time, effort or cost is well used for the intended task or purpose.

Emotional stability is a personality characteristic that relates to a person's ability to cope with stress and manage anxiety in their lives. A person can be rated along the dimension from emotionally stable to neurotic.

Equity can be defined as the belief people have that they are being treated fairly in relation to others and provides people with a sense of what is fair and reasonable. The opposite of equity is inequity.

Ethics are moral principles that govern the behaviour of individuals, groups and organisations.

Eustress is a pleasant stress that accompanies positive events.

Extroversion is a factor influencing human personality and is characterised by a tendency to direct one's energies outwards towards other people's actions and reactions. A central dimension of personality is extroversion to introversion.

False consensus effect involves an overestimation by a person about the degree to which other people agree with him or her. The person assumes that his or her thoughts, values and habits are normal and that other people think in the same way, which enhances his or her self-esteem.

Feedback is a process in which information is provided about past or present performance. Frequent and effective feedback leads to increased productivity and team effectiveness.

First impressions are formed from the information that is initially received about another person, which triggers a person's perceptual set and has an enduring effect.

Groups can be defined as two or more people who interact with each other and in so doing influence and are influenced by each person in the group.

Groupthink occurs when members of a group become so close that disagreement between people becomes less and less likely to take place.

Habituation refers to the fact that people become so used to some stimuli that they do not notice them.

Halo effect occurs when a single characteristic is used to generate an overall positive impression of a person. The opposite of the halo effect is called the rusty halo, horns, trident or devil effect.

Hygiene factors relate to the job environment or context in which the job is done. Hygiene factors such as pay, supervision and working conditions can cause feelings of job dissatisfaction.

Implicit personality theories are general expectations that individuals construct about a person when they know something of their central traits. They are the theories that individuals hold about the personality characteristics that they believe go together.

Innovation is the act of translating an idea or invention into a new product or service.

Insight learning, or problem solving, involves the subject grasping the inner relationship between the elements of a problem. This perceived relationship is essential to finding a solution.

Interactionist perspective on conflict views conflict as a positive and necessary force. Conflict leads to effective performance and stimulates creativity and innovation.

Interdependence is when individuals or groups rely on each other to achieve adequate work flow and quality of work.

Introversion is a factor influencing human personality and is characterised by a tendency to direct one's energies inwards to one's own thoughts, feelings and ideas. A central dimension of personality is extroversion to introversion.

Job design aims to reduce or overcome sources of dissatisfaction and alienation experienced by employees arising from repetitive and mechanistic tasks. Jobs are made more interesting, satisfying and challenging for employees. A job redesign process may involve job enlargement, job enrichment or job rotation.
Job satisfaction represents people's overall positive and/or negative feelings about their jobs.

Latent learning occurs when the brain acquires knowledge without reinforcement, but does not use it until a later time when that knowledge is required.
Leadership is the process of influencing the activities of group members towards goal achievement.
Learning involves a relatively permanent change in people's actual and potential behaviour.
Locus of control refers to the extent to which individuals believe that they can control events that affect them. A person's 'locus' (Latin for place or location) can be either internal (the person believes that what happens to them is caused by them) or external (the person believes that what happens to them is controlled by environmental factors outside of them).

Management focuses on planning, organising, leading and controlling resources to efficiently and effectively achieve organisational goals.
Memory is an information-processing system that facilitates the retention and retrieval of information.
Mnemonic devices are methods that can be used to give information meaning and aid memory.
Motivation is a force that causes people to engage in behaviour that results in the satisfaction of individual needs. It is the relationship between needs, behaviour aimed at overcoming needs and the achievement of goals.

Neuroticism can be defined as an enduring tendency to experience negative emotional states. A person can be rated along the dimension from emotionally stable to neurotic.
Noise refers to any disturbance in the process of communication.
Norms are standards against which the appropriateness of behaviour is judged.

Openness to experience is a factor influencing human personality and is characterised by a person's effectiveness at incorporating new experiences into their understanding of the world.

Operant/Skinnerian conditioning contends that an association is made between behaviour and the consequences that result from engaging in the behaviour. Learning occurs through a method of rewards and punishments for behaviour.

Organisational behaviour (OB) is the study of organisations and the people who work in them. It aims to achieve a better understanding of human behaviour in the workplace in order to enhance the effectiveness of organisations.

Organisational change is a structured approach used by organisations to ensure the successful implementation of change. This involves moving individuals, groups and organisations from their current state to a desired future state.

Organisational citizenship behaviour (OCB) is a type of behaviour demonstrated by employees that results from personal choice rather than a job description and that goes beyond requirements and makes a positive contribution to the organisation.

Organisational commitment concerns a person's identification with and attachment to the organisation.

Organisational culture is the set of shared mental assumptions held by people in an organisation. It defines and gives meaning to appropriate behaviour for various situations.

Organisations are arrangements of people who work together to achieve collective goals in a controlled manner.

Overload occurs when employees are expected to complete more tasks than their time and/or ability allow. It may result in employees feeling under pressure and experiencing stress.

Perception is the selection, organisation and interpretation of information from the environment. It results in a meaningful understanding of the world.

Perceptual distortions, or biases, result from the subjective nature of the process of perception and affect the way an individual perceives a stimulus; examples include stereotypes and the halo effect.

Perceptual set is an individual's predisposition to respond in a particular way, or a perceptual expectancy, which influences people's evaluations of others in many social contexts.

Perceptual threshold is the boundary between the sensory information that people can and cannot detect.

Performance appraisal is an evaluation of an employee's work behaviour. The employee's performance may be compared to predetermined standards. The results of the appraisal are documented and used to provide feedback.

Person perception is the process by which individuals obtain, store and recall information about other people in order to make judgements about them.

Personality is a stable set of characteristics that affects the way a person thinks, feels and behaves and can be used to understand the similarities and differences between people.

Pluralist perspective on conflict asserts that conflict is to be expected in organisations as they are made up of different people and groups. Conflict is believed to be a normal occurrence and should be managed, not eliminated.

Political science is the study of the ways in which political power is achieved and used in countries. It focuses on the processes, principles and structures of government and political institutions.

Productivity is a measure of the efficiency of a person, machine, factory or system in transforming inputs into outputs.

Projection is a psychological defence mechanism that causes a person to unconsciously reject attributes about themselves that they believe to be unacceptable and to ascribe them to other people or objects in the world around them.

Psychology is the scientific study of mental processes and behaviour and provides an understanding of individuals and groups.

Radical perspective on conflict views conflict as an inevitable result of capitalism. Revolutionary change is required to dismantle the capitalist system and redistribute the power to produce a classless society.

Recruitment is the process of searching for and obtaining applicants for available jobs in organisations.

Reinforcement follows a specific response and can be either positive or negative. Positive reinforcement produces pleasant consequences and strengthens behaviour. Negative reinforcement involves the removal of an unfavourable event or outcome after the display of behaviour.

Reliability refers to extent of the consistency of a measure. A test is reliable when the same result is achieved repeatedly.

Resistance to change is an emotional and/or behavioural response made by individuals and groups when they perceive that a change that is taking place may threaten their current situation.

Role ambiguity occurs when an individual is uncertain as to what is expected of him or her in a particular role, the expectations of other people and the exact nature of the job.

Role conflict occurs when expectations about a role contradict each other.

Selection is the process of obtaining and using information about job applicants in order to identify the candidates that should be hired to fill particular positions in organisations.

Selective attention causes people to constantly and actively select stimuli that are interesting and/or important and to filter out information that is not relevant. This prevents the bombardment of the senses.

Self-actualisation is the achievement of potential, self-fulfilment and becoming everything that a person is capable of becoming.

Self-concept is the knowledge and understanding that people have about themselves. It is closely associated with a person's self-esteem.

Self-efficacy refers to a person's evaluation about whether they can successfully acquire new knowledge and skills.

Self-esteem refers to a person's evaluation of their self-worth and has a significant influence on behaviour.

Self-fulfilling prophecy is a prediction that directly or indirectly causes itself to become true. A positive or negative strongly held belief, expectation or prophecy may in itself influence people to react in such a manner as to fulfil the prophecy.

Sensation is the immediate and direct response of the stimulation of the sensory receptors, such as the eye, ear and nose.

Shaping behaviour involves systematically reinforcing aspects of behaviour to achieve desired results.

Social learning theory emphasises the importance of observing and modelling the behaviours, attitudes and emotional reactions of other people.

Social loafing is a tendency for group members to exert less effort in a large group than they would when working alone.

Socialisation is the process by which individuals acquire the knowledge, language, social skills and values needed to conform to the norms and roles required for integration into a group or community.

Sociology is the scientific study of the development, structure and functioning of human society.

Stereotypes are generalised beliefs about a person or group of people that may or may not accurately reflect reality.

Stimulus is something that can evoke or elicit a response. People, objects, events or occurrences in the environment can act as a stimulus that can influence the behaviour of an organism. The plural of stimulus is stimuli.

Stress is an individual's response to an excessive level of psychological or physical pressure.

Teamwork involves a small group of individuals with complementary skills harmonising their contribution and working towards a common goal for which they are collectively accountable.

Type A personality is a set of characteristics relating to an individual's resilience to stress that include being impatient, excessively time-conscious, highly competitive and aggressive. These characteristics affect an individual's susceptibility to stress-related illnesses.

Type B personality is a set of characteristics relating to an individual's resilience to stress that include being relaxed, easy-going, unpressured and confident. These characteristics affect an individual's susceptibility to stress-related illnesses.

Underload occurs if a person has too little to do and too much time to do it. The consequences of underload include boredom, apathy and a lack of participation.

Unitarist perspective on conflict maintains that harmony and unity are the natural state in an organisation. Conflict is believed to be an abnormal occurrence and is negative and damaging.

Validity is the extent to which a test measures that which it claims to measure. A test must be valid in order for the results to be accurately applied and interpreted.

Withdrawal behaviours are actions undertaken by an employee who has become physically and/or psychologically disengaged from the organisation. Physical withdrawal behaviours include lateness, absenteeism and turnover. Psychological withdrawal behaviours include inputting a minimal effort on the job, passive compliance, lack of creativity and presenteeism.

Work–life balance refers to the division of time and effort between a person's employment position and private life.